Presented to:

....

From:

....

Date:

....

Devotions & Prayers for a Courageous Heart

She Will Persevere

BARBOUR PUBLISHING

ISBN 979-8-89151-119-4

Text originally appeared in the following books: *Nevertheless, She Believed*; *Nevertheless, She Had Hope for the Future*; *Nevertheless, She Was Chosen*; and *Nevertheless, She Was Courageous*. All published by Barbour Publishing.

Published by Barbour Publishing, Inc., 1810 Barbour Drive, Uhrichsville, Ohio 44683, www.barbourbooks.com

Our mission is to inspire the world with the life-changing message of the Bible.

ecpa Member of the Evangelical Christian Publishers Association

Printed in China.

Introduction

You have everything you need to persevere, to endure any circumstance, to be strong and courageous.

But it's not because of your own strength or resolve or stubbornness. It's not because you are powerful or invincible or more capable than the next person. Instead, you can stand firm through the storms of life because of the almighty grace and perfection and forgiveness of Jesus Christ.

Let your faith be your stronghold and let the truth of God's Word fully saturate your heart as you read the devotions in this book and learn how to keep going, keep thriving, and keep pushing ahead in godly perseverance.

Let us strip off every weight that slows us down, especially the sin that so easily trips us up. And let us run with endurance the race God has set before us. We do this by keeping our eyes on Jesus, the champion who initiates and perfects our faith. Because of the joy awaiting him, he endured the cross, disregarding its shame. Now he is seated in the place of honor beside God's throne.

HEBREWS 12:1–2 NLT

"Be strong. Take courage. Don't be intimidated. . . . God, your God, is striding ahead of you. He's right there with you. He won't let you down; he won't leave you."

DEUTERONOMY 31:6 MSG

Day 1

A Transformed Mind

Don't copy the behavior and customs of this world, but let God transform you into a new person by changing the way you think. Then you will learn to know God's will for you, which is good and pleasing and perfect.

ROMANS 12:2 NLT

Your thoughts matter to God. Did you know that it's possible to direct your thoughts? If you notice that you're thinking negatively, at that very moment, purposefully switch your thoughts to focus on something positive. Over time you can create a healthy habit of positive thinking. As believers, we want to align our thoughts with the truth of God's Word. He has so much wisdom to share with us about how to think and how to relate to others. He does not want us to be intimidated by toxic people or the toxic thinking of our own selves at times.

Lord, highlight any wrong thinking in me. Show me how to align my thoughts with Yours.

Day 2

Gifts

In his grace, God has given us different gifts for doing certain things well.
ROMANS 12:6 NLT

You are a unique woman. Your blend of experience, talents, and personality are gifts you can share with the world. But when you choose to put your faith in God, you also receive "spiritual" gifts. God gives you these abilities so you can help others see Him more clearly. By using gifts such as teaching, serving, or encouragement, you make faith visible. Ask God to help you understand and use the gifts He's so graciously given to you.

Lord, we often question how You've made us. Why aren't we good at this? Why do we struggle so much with that? Help us to rest in who we are in Christ, knowing that both our struggles and our gifts are from You, to be used for Your glory. Amen.

Day 3

Live Like He Loves You

You are holy and loved by Him. Because of this, your new life should be full of loving-pity. You should be kind to others and have no pride. Be gentle and be willing to wait for others. Try to understand other people.

COLOSSIANS 3:12–13 NLV

Jesus died to make us holy. He lived our righteousness because we couldn't, and then He suffered an excruciating death to cover our filth and allow us to walk into eternity unhindered. He rescued us from the jaws of eternal death and gave us abundant life in its place. And because of this great love story for the ages, we should be changed. The knowledge of what He did for us should pierce our sin-shrouded hearts. Try to understand the struggles of others today and gently lift them up through love.

Father, I know You love me. Help me to live out Your love toward others. Amen.

Day 4

Devoted to Ministry

This is how one should regard us, as servants of Christ and stewards of the mysteries of God.

1 CORINTHIANS 4:1 ESV

Ministry is not only done in a church; it is accomplished anywhere we serve another in need. Ministry therefore can happen at a school meeting, in a crowded grocery store, standing in line at the post office, and in many other places.

There are specific types of ministry, of course. Some women minister as nurses in a hospital. Some women serve in ministry as teachers to small children. Some women care for elderly parents or volunteer at the local assisted-living facility or work in the church nursery. Whatever your ministry, do it with a cheerful heart and a focus on loving Him and others.

Dear God, thank You for sending Jesus as the great example of ministry. I want to be like Him. Amen.

Day 5

Changing Direction

Finally, brothers and sisters, whatever is true, whatever is noble, whatever is right, whatever is pure, whatever is lovely, whatever is admirable—if anything is excellent or praiseworthy—think about such things.

PHILIPPIANS 4:8 NIV

It's easy to get off track and think about things we shouldn't—even when we're praying! We start off thinking about something good, and then we easily get distracted by other thoughts and people. The next time you find yourself thinking about something that isn't right, ask Jesus to step into your thoughts and change them! Just speak His name and ask Him to come to your rescue. The name of Jesus has all power in heaven and earth (Philippians 2:10), and just speaking His name can change the direction of your thoughts.

Jesus, Your name is powerful. I pray You will step in and change my thoughts to be pure and true when I'm distracted.

Day 6

Another Morning Sun

*The sun also rises and the sun goes down,
and hastens to the place where it rises.*
ECCLESIASTES 1:5 AMPC

Every day, life begins and ends with the sun, in a manner of speaking. Of course, on some days, the sun isn't visible where we are—it is hidden behind clouds or obscured by inclement weather. But the dawning of a new day is a natural reset button that God built into our world. This is one of the challenges for those who work the night shift; their center of refocus is gone because they work through the hours when our minds were meant to defragment and be restored.

Yesterday may have been horrible. And its pain may still be with you. But God has created today to help you with yesterday. And the shining of the sun is His reminder.

Creator God, thank You for the sun and its brilliant way of reminding me. Amen.

Day 7

Chosen to Forgive

Forgive each other.
COLOSSIANS 3:13 NLV

Three little words. And yet living by their creed can be as formidable as summiting Everest. Someone hurts our feelings, and we grab on to that offense with the tenacity of an emaciated junkyard dog gnawing his last bone. We refuse to let it go. We refuse to forgive. Instead, we play their painful words on a loop in our imagination, breaking open the wound over and over. Somewhere in our pain we forget that we too have been forgiven—probably of much greater offenses. Loved one, your Father in heaven chose you as His prized possession. He forgave you. And He asks you to do the same. Is there someone you need to forgive today?

Father, soften my heart of stone. Help me to gain control over my thoughts and choose to forgive those who have hurt me. In Jesus' name, amen.

Day 8

No Comparison Necessary

We will not compare ourselves with each other as if one of us were better and another worse. We have far more interesting things to do with our lives. Each of us is an original.
GALATIANS 5:26 MSG

When God created each of us, He wove together a wonderful woman unlike any other. But at times it's tempting to gauge how well we're doing by using other women as a measuring stick. Faith offers a different standard. The Bible encourages us to use our abilities in ways that honor God. Some abilities may take center stage while others work quietly in the background. Just do what you can with what you have in ways that make God smile. No comparison necessary.

God, when I see another woman with gifts that I wish I had, help me to turn my envy into praise. Thank You for her. Thank You for making her a light and inspiration to many. Help me to support her in the work You've given her so that You may be glorified even more. Amen.

Day 9

Blossoms

The godly will flourish like palm trees. . . . Even in old age they will still produce fruit; they will remain vital and green.

Psalm 92:12, 14 NLT

As you grow close to God, you blossom spiritually. But this is one flower that will never fade or fall. Your body will age, but spiritually you'll continue to grow stronger and more beautiful. The more time you spend with God, the more your character will begin to resemble His—and the more humble you'll find yourself in His presence. This is exactly the kind of woman God is looking for to do wonderful things in this world.

Dear Lord, You know how I have been struggling with aging lately. You know the aches and pains and limitations You've given me. Please help me to deal gracefully with them. But more importantly, help me to grow closer to You through them. I long for fruit that will last. Amen.

Day 10

The Power of Words

Let everything you say be good and helpful, so that your words will be an encouragement to those who hear them.
EPHESIANS 4:29 NLT

Research tells us women speak about twice as many words as men do each day. That gives us twice as many reasons to pay attention to what we say! It's easy to let whatever pops into our heads pop out of our mouths, but the Bible reminds us that our words have power. We're responsible for how we use that power. Will we hurt or heal? Build up or tear down? Allow faith to help you choose wisely.

Lord, we want our children to learn to control their tongues, but so often we use our tongues without thinking. Forgive us for that hypocrisy. We pray that the words coming out of our mouths would be Your words. We pray for wisdom. We pray for the strength to remain silent. Amen.

Day 11

Worship with Joy

Lift up your hands to the holy place and bless the LORD!

PSALM 134:2 ESV

In developing your reputation, don't forget about worship.

A woman who worships is a woman who has her priorities right. Worship means we understand who is truly worthy, and we offer Him the adoration of our hearts and the obedience of our lives. Worship is a way to give public voice to the thankfulness we should express because of His goodness to us in sending His Son. Worship tells others that we keep first things first.

Being known in your church as a woman who worships is one of the greatest compliments you could receive. Never be ashamed to lift your hands toward the Lord and give Him honor.

Father in heaven, You alone deserve my worship.
I want to be known as a worshipper of You. Amen.

Day 12

A Huge Promise

Don't worry about anything; instead, pray about everything. Tell God what you need, and thank him for all he has done. Then you will experience God's peace, which exceeds anything we can understand. His peace will guard your hearts and minds as you live in Christ Jesus.

PHILIPPIANS 4:6–7 NLT

When you hold worries inside of you, they can actually cause harm to your body. God wants you to bring those fears and worries to Him instead. He promises that when you do that, a very powerful thing happens: He'll give you His peace. It's a peace that doesn't really make sense to anyone else but you and God, no matter what you're facing. He wants you to be thankful instead of stressed, and He alone can help you do that.

God, I pray for Your peace to wash over me as I bring my worries to You. Thank You for always keeping Your promises.

Day 13

From God's Perspective

Has not God chosen those who are poor in the eyes of the world to be rich in faith and to inherit the kingdom he promised those who love him?

James 2:5 NIV

Being rich in faith is the secret to leading an abundant life. That's because faith allows us to see life from God's perspective. We begin to appreciate how much we have instead of focusing on what we think we lack. We understand that what's of eternal worth is more valuable than our net worth. We feel rich, regardless of how much, or how little, we own. True abundance flows from the inside out—from God's hand straight to our hearts.

Dear Father, we are blessed beyond measure—both now and in eternity—because You have given us the immeasurable gift of Your only Son, Jesus Christ. Help us to keep our eyes fixed on that treasure, which will never fade and cannot be taken from us. Amen.

Day 14

Chosen to Love

"You have not chosen Me, I have chosen you.
I have set you apart for the work of bringing in fruit. . . .
This is what I tell you to do: Love each other."
JOHN 15:16–17 NLV

God wants us to make no mistake about the initiator of our relationship with Him. He chose us, not the other way around. He picked you for His kingdom, and He didn't just single you out of a crowd: He created you specifically with love and great detail and set you apart for the work He has prepared for you—the work of showing others Jesus. No one can finish the tasks He has planned for your life quite like you can, because you were made for them. His instructions are simple: love. Go out and show someone Christ's love today.

Lord, show me the work of love You have earmarked for me today. Amen.

Day 15

You Belong to Him

"If the world hates you, you know it hated Me before it hated you. If you belonged to the world, the world would love you as its own. You do not belong to the world. I have chosen you out of the world and the world hates you."
John 15:18–19 NLV

Be careful about fitting in too well with the world's culture. If you're embraced by a godless society and blend like a chameleon into its masses, it should be a warning sign to you. Jesus said that the world would reject His followers with the same animosity it showed Him. But don't be discouraged! You belong to Him. He has chosen you right out of this world and into a better one—the eternal kingdom of His Father.

Father God, it hurts when the world hates me because I love You, but this trial has a silver lining—it proves that I belong to You. Amen.

Day 16

Make Some Music

Give thanks to the Lord with the lyre;
sing praises to Him with the harp of ten strings.
Psalm 33:2 AMPC

Stringed instruments were common in the days when the Bible was written. Just like in Appalachia, there was, no doubt, a great assortment of musical items made with strings. Who was the first person to discover that blowing into a hollow tube or plucking a taut string or hitting a stretched piece of skin with a mallet would make music? Someone did, and music-making has been part of human life ever since.

When you get up tomorrow, invest in your everyday life by turning on uplifting, Christ-centered music to remind you that there is hope and joy for your next twenty-four hours.

Lord, You created music for our enjoyment and for Your glory. Thank You for this rich gift. Amen.

Day 17

Steady Me

Provide me with the insight that comes only from your Word. Give my request your personal attention, rescue me on the terms of your promise. . . . Every order you've given is right. Put your hand out and steady me since I've chosen to live by your counsel.

PSALM 119:170–173 MSG

The Bible tells us that God gives us wisdom and insight, and that He gives it freely without finding fault (James 1:5–7). The only requirement is that you trust Him. Believe that God's will is best and that He will lead and guide you in making decisions that align with His purposes.

God wants you to hear His voice and know His will for you. He has promised in His Word that if you seek Him, you *will* find Him—if you seek with all of your heart (Jeremiah 29:13).

Lord, may I go to You for wisdom and insight. Steady my heart and mind in You alone.

Day 18

Eternally Present

God's love, though, is ever and always, eternally present to all who fear him, making everything right for them and their children as they follow his Covenant ways and remember to do whatever he said.

Psalm 103:18 MSG

Nothing can separate us from the love of God (Romans 8:39). Nothing. Because of Jesus and His triumphant work on the cross, we will never be separated from God's love again. He is constantly going ahead of us and behind us, rewriting our story with "mercy's pen," as a popular worship song reminds us. Instead of worrying about the next dose of hardship coming your way, allow yourself to rest along the journey, viewing life as a great adventure with Jesus. He is eternally present with you, He loves you, and He is always at work in your life.

Thank You for this great adventure, Lord.
It's not always easy, but I know You are always with me.

Day 19

Personal, Loving God

"Because I am God, your personal God, The Holy of Israel, your Savior. I paid a huge price for you. . . . That's how much you mean to me! That's how much I love you! I'd sell off the whole world to get you back, trade the creation just for you."

Isaiah 43:4 MSG

Do you believe God loves you this much? You are of great worth to God. He would trade the whole world to get you back! He is your own personal God, with you always, going ahead of you forever. How does that make you feel? God wants your friends and family to know this too. Ask Him for courage to share His love with others.

Thank You for Your amazing love for me, God. Please grant me the courage to love others and to share with them where my love comes from.

Day 20

Exceeded Expectations

"The thief's purpose is to steal and kill and destroy.
My purpose is to give them a rich and satisfying life."
JOHN 10:10 NLT

In Jesus' day, the people of Israel were looking for the Messiah promised in scripture. They believed this Savior would restore Israel to its former power and prosperity. Jesus didn't meet their expectations—He exceeded them. Jesus offered them an abundance of riches that couldn't be stolen or decrease in value—true treasures like joy, peace, forgiveness, and eternal life. Jesus offers these same treasures to you. All you need to do is place your faith in Him.

We want what You want, Lord. We want to desire the things You desire. Forgive us for being goaded and deceived by the world into wanting the things that it offers. We ask for the Holy Spirit to fill us so we will desire everything that pleases You. Amen.

Day 21

Fresh from His Hand

They gathered it every morning, each as much as he needed, for when the sun became hot it melted. . . . The house of Israel called the bread manna; it was like coriander seed, white, and it tasted like wafers made with honey.

Exodus 16:21, 31 AMPC

Do you have a morning ritual? Most of us do. We roll out of bed after turning off the alarm and shuffle to the bathroom or to the kitchen. For many of us, the morning routine probably involves pouring a cup of coffee from the coffeepot or brewing an individual cup. Some add cream, some add sugar, and a few hearty souls drink it black.

Our morning refreshment surely doesn't compare to the manna God gave to the ancient Hebrews. But every good thing in our morning should remind us again that blessings come from His hand, fresh every day.

O God, I delight in Your daily provisions for me, even down to my cup of coffee. Amen.

Day 22

A New Start

But there is another power within me that is at war with my mind. This power makes me a slave to the sin that is still within me. Oh, what a miserable person I am! Who will free me from this life that is dominated by sin and death? Thank God! The answer is in Jesus Christ our Lord.

Romans 7:23–25 NLT

You find yourself slipping into old patterns, thinking negatively about yourself or others, feeling down. . .what then? Romans 7 echoes this same kind of humanness. The answer is the start of the very next chapter: "So now there is no condemnation for those who belong to Christ Jesus. And because you belong to him, the power of the life-giving Spirit has freed you from the power of sin that leads to death" (Romans 8:1–2 NLT). You can start again.

Jesus, thank You for the truth that I am not condemned. Please give me the power to start again.

Day 23

Help for His Chosen

"The Helper (Holy Spirit) will tell about Me when He comes. I will send Him to you from the Father. He is the Spirit of Truth and comes from the Father."

JOHN 15:26 NLV

When your courage wanes, remember the helper. You don't have to do life all alone; you have help. The Holy Spirit moved into your heart the moment you believed in Jesus' death and resurrection. Don't waste this resource! The Holy Spirit can teach, strengthen, and equip you with everything you need. And you're His witness in this world to spread the amazing news. Has Jesus changed you, given you hope, assisted you in struggles, or helped you to solve problems? Tell someone.

God, thank You for sending the Holy Spirit to help me. Teach me to rely on You, and show me who I can tell today about what You've done in my life. In Jesus' name, amen.

Day 24

A Dumb Ox

When I was beleaguered and bitter, totally consumed by envy, I was totally ignorant, a dumb ox in your very presence. I'm still in your presence, but you've taken my hand. You wisely and tenderly lead me, and then you bless me.

PSALM 73:21–24 MSG

Have you ever felt like a dumb ox in certain situations? This comical word picture explains some of what we may have felt over our ignorance in the past. But once we invite Jesus to take our hand, everything changes. He tenderly leads us and fills us with His wisdom as we're able to take it in. As we grow in our relationship with Jesus, He blesses us immensely with His presence and His love. We no longer have to feel like a dumb animal. He takes away our shame and gives blessing instead.

Thank You, Jesus, for taking away all my shame and blessing me instead.

Day 25

A Story to Tell

It is with your heart that you believe and are justified, and it is with your mouth that you profess your faith and are saved.

ROMANS 10:10 NIV

For some people, faith is a very private part of their lives. But you have a story to tell that others need to hear. Sharing how God is at work in your life gives others permission to ask spiritual questions. Don't worry about not having all the answers. You can't. An infinite God will always be bigger than our finite minds can comprehend. But saying aloud what you believe is part of living and growing in your faith.

Dear Lord, I need Your help to grow in this area. I am so afraid of what other people think of me and so worried about not having all the answers. Forgive me for not trusting Your Spirit to speak through me. Help me to start, even in some small way, today. Amen.

Day 26

Completely!

The Spirit makes us sure God will accept us because of our faith in Christ.
GALATIANS 5:5 CEV

God accepts you completely. You don't need to clean up your language, change your lifestyle, or step inside of a church. Once you put your faith in Jesus, things between you and God are made right. Period. But acceptance is only the first step in this relationship. As God's Spirit continues working in your heart, He gives you the desire and strength you need to mature into who you were created to be: an amazing woman whose character reflects God's.

Dear Lord, we praise You that because of the perfect sacrifice of Jesus, we are acceptable to You in any condition—even when we're broken, weary, filthy, and crooked. We praise You that You don't discard us or dismiss us as worthless. Instead, You make us new. In praise and thanksgiving, amen.

Day 27

Divine Breath

The Spirit of God has made me, and the breath of the Almighty gives me life.

Job 33:4 ESV

If you've ever had to have your oxygen level checked for medical reasons, you know that there is a healthy percentage at which it should be detectable in your bloodstream. The body needs the energy from oxygen in order to live.

The Bible tells us that God breathed living air through His Spirit into Adam's lungs, and symbolically every human being since has been a recipient of that divine breath.

Job tells us that our daily oxygen comes from the Almighty. It is one of His daily gifts and a reason that we can have hope. He is the life giver.

Jehovah God, thank You for breath and life. I praise You for Your marvelous creation. Amen.

Day 28

Happy Heart, Joyful Mind

A happy heart is good medicine and a joyful mind causes healing, but a broken spirit dries up the bones.

Proverbs 17:22 AMP

Stress is hard on a body, physically and mentally. Extended and unrelenting stress can cause heart problems and even death. God does not want us to carry all of that on our shoulders. It's too much. But life is hard, and traumatic things do happen. Does God want you just to sweep your troubles under the rug and paste on a happy, fake face? Surely not. Jesus invites you to come to Him with everything. As you give Him permission to heal your hurts and heartaches, He supernaturally gives you rest and peace. As you linger in His very presence, He fills you with His joy that brings healing.

Jesus, I bring You my heartaches and my worries. I want Your healing presence in my life.

Day 29

Sound Sleep

The L*ORD* *is your protector, and he won't go to sleep or let you stumble.*

PSALM 121:3 CEV

For small children, bedtime can be a scary time. They may be afraid of the dark, of monsters lurking under their beds, or of bad dreams disturbing their slumber. Bedtime prayers can help calm their fears. They can calm yours as well. Knowing God never sleeps can help you sleep more soundly. If you're in the dark about a certain situation, if "monsters" are threatening your peace, take your concerns to God. It's never too late to call out to Him.

Lord, usually when it's bedtime, all I think about is how fast I can lay my head on my pillow and shut out the cares of the day. Forgive me for forgetting You. Help me, instead, to remember to pause and turn my mind toward You in praise before I go to sleep. Amen.

Day 30

A Favorite Lullaby

I think about you, God, before I go to sleep,
and my thoughts turn to you during the night.
PSALM 63:6 CEV

Sleep can be elusive, particularly during certain seasons of a woman's life. If 2 a.m. feedings, the throes of menopause, or simply mentally sorting through the demands of daily life are keeping you awake, set aside your frustration. Picture yourself pulling up the blanket of darkness, settling into the silence of night. Then turn your thoughts to God. Pour out your problems or lift up your praises. Ask God for refreshment and renewal. Allow God's voice to become your favorite lullaby.

Thank You, Lord, that when sleep is elusive, You are not. You are right there beside us in the darkest, loneliest, most anxious part of the night, ready to offer comfort, conviction, and companionship. Our sleeping and rising are in Your hands. Teach us to rest in that. Amen.

Day 31

Faith into Action

Offer your bodies to him as a living sacrifice, pure and pleasing. That's the most sensible way to serve God.

ROMANS 12:1 CEV

The most important choice you'll ever make is whether to serve God or yourself. The good news is that by choosing to serve God, you wind up doing what's best for yourself as well. Caring for the body God has given you is one way of serving Him. That includes eating a healthy diet, exercising regularly, getting annual check-ups, and using your body in ways that honor God and others. It's just one more way of putting your faith into action.

Lord, thank You for the amazing body You have given me. Every morning I wake up and can see the sunlight, hear birds singing, and walk to the coffeepot! Not everyone is so blessed. Give me wisdom and discipline to take care of myself so I can serve You for many more years. Amen.

Day 32

Celebrate!

We remember before our God and Father your work produced by faith, your labor prompted by love, and your endurance inspired by hope in our Lord Jesus Christ.

1 THESSALONIANS 1:3 NIV

When you work hard toward completing a goal, accomplishing what you've set out to do is something worth celebrating. When your accomplishment is fueled by faith, you can be certain you'll never celebrate alone. God sees the time, energy, and heart you put into your work. Better yet, He adds His own power to your efforts. This means that with God, you can accomplish things you could never do solely on your own. That's something truly worth celebrating—with God!

Lord, thank You for blessing the work of my hands. Thank You for the plans You have for my future, plans to prosper me and not to harm me. I know I can trust You to carry them to completion. I look forward—with joy!—to what You will do. Amen.

Day 33

Healthy Routine

Everyone also to whom God has given wealth and possessions and power to enjoy them, and to accept his lot and rejoice in his toil—this is the gift of God.

Ecclesiastes 5:19 ESV

Often we grow bored with routine, of doing the same things over and over, of going on monotonously with the repeated motions of everyday life.

But routine is also one of God's gifts that remind us we have hope in the everyday. Routine symbolizes that we have stability in life and some measure of safety, as well as the means to do the same thing tomorrow that we did today.

Routine is healthy for our minds and for our budgets, keeping us from random decisions and from unwise spending and keeping us steady in the channel of life.

Creator God, thank You for giving me the resources to have a daily routine. I'm grateful. Amen.

Day 34

The Mind of Christ

Who ever knows what you're thinking and planning except you yourself? The same with God—except that he not only knows what he's thinking, but he lets us in on it.

1 CORINTHIANS 2:11–12 MSG

The New Living Translation paraphrases verse 12: "And we have received God's Spirit (not the world's spirit), so we can know the wonderful things God has freely given us."

Verse 16 in *The Message* says, "Isaiah's question, 'Is there anyone around who knows God's Spirit, anyone who knows what he is doing?' has been answered: Christ knows, and we have Christ's Spirit."

Why is all of this so extremely important? Because without God's Spirit alive in us, we couldn't possibly know or follow the ways of Christ. But because He is. . .we can!

Lord, I'm so thankful that You've given me Your Spirit. Without Him, I would never be able to go against the strong pull of the world to follow You and know Your ways.

Day 35

Words and Thoughts

May these words of my mouth and this meditation of my heart be pleasing in your sight, Lord, my Rock and my Redeemer.

Psalm 19:14 NIV

Your thoughts and your words are very important to God. Take a look at what the Bible says: "A good person produces good things from the treasury of a good heart, and an evil person produces evil things from the treasury of an evil heart. What you say flows from what is in your heart" (Luke 6:45 NLT).

Basically, what goes in is what comes out. If the things you are taking in (entertainment choices, social media posts, conversations. . .) are honoring to God, you are storing good things in your heart. And that's what will come out. The opposite is also true. What are you filling your heart and mind with?

Lord, I want to honor You with what I'm taking into my mind and heart.

Day 36

Letting Go

"Do not remember the former things, or ponder the things of the past. Listen carefully, I am about to do a new thing, now it will spring forth; will you not be aware of it? I will even put a road in the wilderness, rivers in the desert."

Isaiah 43:18–19 AMP

Like all of us, you probably have some things in your past you'd really like to forget. But heated conversations and failures often replay themselves in your mind. Jesus doesn't want you to keep carrying those burdens around. You can't fix everything, and you certainly can't fix other people. But you can fix your mind on Christ: "Forgetting what is behind and straining toward what is ahead, I press on toward the goal to win the prize for which God has called me heavenward in Christ Jesus" (Philippians 3:13–14 NIV).

Jesus, please help me to let go of past failures and press on in faith.

Day 37

Courageous Footsteps

"Blessed is she who has believed that the Lord would fulfill his promises to her!"

LUKE 1:45 NIV

In Jesus' day, women had fewer opportunities to stretch their wings creatively and professionally than they do today. That didn't stop them from holding tightly to God's promises and stepping out to act on what they believed. You can follow in their courageous footsteps. Whatever you believe God wants you to do, big or small, don't hold back. Today, take at least one step toward your goal. With God's help, you'll accomplish everything He's set out for you to do.

Dear Lord, sometimes I'm afraid to keep walking toward the goals You have planted in my heart. The way seems long and hard. . .and I am still so far from where I long to be. Yet I know that You are with me. Help me to take a step forward in faith today. Amen.

Day 38

Perfect Senses

Then the Lord asked Moses, "Who makes a person's mouth?
Who decides whether people speak or do not speak,
hear or do not hear, see or do not see? Is it not I, the Lord?"

Exodus 4:11 NLT

As we rise every morning to face a new hope, an important one is the often-discounted joy of having five senses—seeing, hearing, tasting, smelling, and touching. These ways in which we interact with the world around us remind us that our God wants us to take pleasure both in nature and in other human beings.

When a physical sense is lost because of an accident or genetic abnormality, the others become heightened to help make up the difference. Considering the genius of our Creator, we should start each new day in awe of our senses that connect us to the world and to each other.

Thank You, God, for making ears, eyes, nose, mouth, and skin. Your goodness gives me hope. Amen.

Day 39

Answers

"This is GOD's Message, the God who made earth, made it livable and lasting, known everywhere as GOD: 'Call to me and I will answer you. I'll tell you marvelous and wondrous things that you could never figure out on your own.' "

JEREMIAH 33:3 MSG

When you talk to God, He wants to have a real conversation with you. Praying is not about sending a wish list to heaven. It's telling God how you feel about certain things and then listening for His answers. God answers us in lots of ways. He can speak to us through just about anything (one time He even spoke through a donkey! Look up the story here: Numbers 22:28–30). He loves to speak through His Word, through worship songs, through the love of another Jesus follower, through His creation—God's ways are limitless. The next time you pray, sit and listen for God to answer. What is He telling you?

Help me to hear and understand Your answers, Lord.

Day 40

Chosen to Bear Fruit

"I am the true Vine. My Father is the One Who cares for the Vine. He takes away any branch in Me that does not give fruit. Any branch that gives fruit, He cuts it back so it will give more fruit."

John 15:1–2 NLV

An untended fruit tree is a gnarled mess of branches and small, blemished fruit. But pruning will encourage both growth and fruit production. Jesus says that we are like this fruit tree. And our loving heavenly Father is the one wielding the clippers. At times His gentle rebukes for sinful behavior and correction for wrong attitudes can pinch. But He knows that a pruned tree will give more fruit. His love will flow more freely from you when you are shaped by His hand.

Father, even when Your pruning is difficult or painful, I want to yield to Your ways. Make me more fruitful. Amen.

Day 41

The Big Picture

See how Abraham's faith and deeds worked together.
He proved his faith was real by what he did.
JAMES 2:22 CEV

Abraham wholeheartedly believed in God's power and love. So when God told Abraham to sacrifice his long-awaited son, Abraham prepared to do exactly what God had asked. Surely Abraham had questions. He didn't know how everything would turn out. In the end, God saved Isaac and commended Abraham's faith. Serving God isn't always an easy path. You may not see the big picture behind what you're asked to do. But you can trust that God's plan for you is good.

Dear Lord, Abraham said, when asked to sacrifice Isaac, "God himself will provide the lamb" (Genesis 22:8 NIV). You provided then, and You provide now. Jesus is that perfect lamb, sacrificed for our sins. And because You raised Your only Son from the dead, we can trust You with our lives. Amen.

Day 42

Under Control

For God did not give us a spirit of timidity or cowardice or fear, but [He has given us a spirit] of power and of love and of sound judgment and personal discipline.

2 TIMOTHY 1:7 AMP

Have you ever excused your own poor behavior by saying, "That's just the way I am"? God's Spirit tells a different story about who you are. Through faith, you have the ability to live a life characterized by discipline and self-control. But the choice to live that life is up to you. Consider the "character flaws" you see in your life. Ask God to help you get these areas under control—one thought, word, or action at a time.

Dear Lord, I blame others for my failures. I speak hastily and without love. I judge without knowledge. I think of myself first. I want to change these things about myself, and I know that change can only come through Your Spirit. Please, Lord, work in me. Amen.

Day 43

God, Your God, Is Striding ahead of You

"It is the LORD *who goes before you.*
He will be with you; he will not leave you or
forsake you. Do not fear or be dismayed."
DEUTERONOMY 31:8 ESV

Think about the last time you felt fear—deep, alarming fear. What caused it? A noise in the night? A child in danger? Bring to mind a memory of fear that you've had. Why was it so troubling to you? As you begin your prayer time, ask Jesus what He wants you to know about this memory. Where was He when you were so worried? Sit with this memory in your mind and begin to pray. Ask Jesus for His truth in the situation. Write down what He tells you.

Jesus, I bring You my memories and my fears.
Please increase my faith as I begin to understand
that You will never leave me nor forsake me.

Day 44

Made for His Purpose

"Before I formed you in the womb I knew you,
before you were born I set you apart;
I appointed you as a prophet to the nations."

JEREMIAH 1:5 NIV

Your life is neither a cosmic coincidence nor an accident of nature. Quite the opposite, in fact. The Creator of the universe knew you before you were born. He has been planning your life for generations. He carefully crafted your personality and talents; He chose your ancestors and the timing of your birth. Even when it feels as if your existence is insignificant, know that your life has meaning and purpose in God's kingdom. Your heavenly Father sees you and knows every graceful arc and rough edge of your personality—and He loves you. Ask Him today what you should do.

Father, thank You for knitting me together with such careful detail. Show me Your will for my life. Amen.

Day 45

Overflowing with Hope

We live by faith, not by sight.
2 CORINTHIANS 5:7 NIV

Faith changes how we see the world. From all appearances, your circumstances may seem daunting. Your opportunities limited. Your future set in stone. But when you place your faith in God instead of in what you see, your heart can't help but overflow with hope. God's power is at work behind the scenes. He's working in both you and your circumstances. He promises to bring something good out of every situation, no matter how things may look on the outside.

Father, I am so grateful that I don't have to judge based on appearances—You look past appearances and so can I. No matter how dark the way seems or how weak and weary I feel, I know that You are—right now—working all things for good. With praise, amen.

Day 46

Steadfast Seasons

He changes the times and the seasons; He removes kings and sets up kings. He gives wisdom to the wise and knowledge to those who have understanding!

DANIEL 2:21 AMPC

One of the greatest reminders that we have hope is the changing of the seasons.

After the great flood, God promised Noah that the springtime and harvest and summer and winter would not perish as long as the earth remained (Genesis 8:22). We may rest in that fact, reveling in the fiery colors of fall and the tranquility of winter, the green flurry of spring and the bright warmth of summer. The seasons are set into the cycle of earth, which He upholds.

Whatever the season outside your window today, find hope in the fact that it has appeared like clockwork, on His schedule.

God of heaven, the seasons remind me of Your steadfast truth and unfailing promises. Thank You for hope. Amen.

Day 47

A God Who Fights, a Dad Who Carries

"The LORD your God is going ahead of you.
He will fight for you, just as you saw him do in Egypt."
DEUTERONOMY 1:30 NLT

The Message paraphrases this verse this way: "GOD, your God, is leading the way; he's fighting for you. You saw with your own eyes what he did for you in Egypt; you saw what he did in the wilderness, how GOD, your God, carried you as a father carries his child, carried you the whole way until you arrived here."

Any good father, if his beloved child is in danger, will fight to free her from an enemy and carry her to safety. Our God does this too. Have you needed a champion in your life? Can you picture Jesus fighting for you and carrying you in His arms?

Thank You for being a good, good Father to me!

Day 48

Cling to Him

"Serve only the Lord your God and fear him alone. Obey his commands, listen to his voice, and cling to him."
Deuteronomy 13:4 NLT

In a "take charge of your destiny" world, trusting God can be a hard sell. It's vital to keep our perspective in check. When we're shopping online for a new pair of boots, we read every review to discover their performance in all types of weather. And God doesn't ask us to trust Him blindly without evidence either. The Bible is loaded with positive reviews from faithful people who chose to follow His leading, even when things weren't looking so good. Allow God to lead, even in your mess, and listen for His voice. Never let go of the one who sees both ends of eternity.

Father, teach me to trust You more. In Jesus' name, amen.

Day 49

Contribute What You Can

Everyone to whom much was given, of him much will be required, and from him to whom they entrusted much, they will demand the more.
LUKE 12:48 ESV

When we were little, we might have heard someone say, "God has a wonderful plan for your life."

Every single person was designed to contribute beautifully to the earthly template of existence. Some people cannot use their gifts because of the tragedy of genetic abnormality or devastating injury, and some cannot contribute because their very lives were taken through abortion.

But on those who are living and well is the responsibility to use our gifts well for the glory of our Creator and the good of others.

I trust You today, Lord, to come alongside me as I use the gifts You've ordained me to have. Amen.

Day 50

Made Like Us

For this reason he had to be made like them, fully human in every way, in order that he might become a merciful and faithful high priest in service to God, and that he might make atonement for the sins of the people. Because he himself suffered when he was tempted, he is able to help those who are being tempted.

HEBREWS 2:17–18 NIV

God chose to come to earth in human form to be made like us. To understand what it's like to be human. To be able to fully take our place and remove our sins. Because He was fully human while being fully God, He can help. He can comfort. Our God is not one who wants to remain as a distant high king, out of touch with the commoners. He wants a very personal relationship with each one of us. He lowered Himself to our level so that we could have personal and continual access to Him.

Thank You for becoming one of us, Jesus.
Thank You for Your comfort.

Day 51

God of the Impossible

"With God nothing is ever impossible."
LUKE 1:37 AMPC

Sometimes life works itself into a tangled knot. We can't see the way forward, and much like the Israelites trapped on the shores of the Red Sea, we're tempted to despair. But God has a history of making ways through impassable problems. Keep your faith alive! God can and will show up in your desperate circumstances if you wait for Him. After all, He has big plans for you. Put your mustard-seed-sized faith in the God of the ages, and He'll move the mountains standing in the way of His plans.

Lord, when I don't see a way to mend a friendship, overcome a devastating loss, or accomplish an out-of-reach goal, help me to trust in You. You created the world from nothing and raised the dead to life, so my problems are not too much for You. Amen.

Day 52

Clothe Your Heart

What matters is not your outer appearance—
the styling of your hair, the jewelry you wear,
the cut of your clothes—but your inner disposition.
1 PETER 3:3–4 MSG

For many women, getting dressed is a bit like painting a portrait. They put themselves together in a way that reflects how they want others to see them. Successful? Confident? Youthful? A bit of a rebel? Who you are on the inside speaks much louder than what you wear on the outside. As you allow God, through faith, to clothe your heart in love and compassion, you'll automatically become more attractive. You'll draw others toward you and God, regardless of what you are wearing.

Dear Lord, thank You for reminding us that what we look like is not who we are. You see the inside, where it counts. Help us to hold lightly the things that will fade and to work at making truly beautiful the things that will last forever. Amen.

Day 53

Use It for God

But the midwives feared God and did not do as the king of Egypt commanded them, but let the male children live. . . . So God dealt well with the midwives. And the people multiplied and grew very strong. And because the midwives feared God, he gave them families.

EXODUS 1:17, 20–21 ESV

In the time when God's people were in captivity in Egypt, there were two very busy Hebrew midwives—Shiphrah and Puah. They dared to defy the Pharoah's decree about killing the Hebrew baby boys. And because of that, God blessed them and gave them their own families.

These women used their abilities to bless God's people and to protect life and to advance God's plans. We may use their example to encourage us to do the same.

God of all, may my stewardship of my abilities fulfill Your purposes. Amen.

Day 54

Beyond Your Imagination

God is able to do much more than we ask or think through His power working in us.
Ephesians 3:20 NLV

The New International Version says that God can do "immeasurably more" than what you could imagine. When God's power is at work within you, the possibilities are beyond your imagination. Whatever problem you are facing right now—big or small—God cares. As you pray and think about it, don't put God in a box, assuming that there's no way out or that there is only one right answer. He is always going before you. And His response just might be beyond your understanding and your wildest imagination. Things aren't always what they seem. If you feel disappointed in God's answers to your prayers, look outside the box. God is always, always working everything out for your good.

Lord, help me to trust that You are working everything out in the best possible way.

Day 55

Attractive

Better to be patient than powerful; better to have self-control than to conquer a city.
PROVERBS 16:32 NLT

Self-control is attractive to others and to God. That's because self-control reflects God's own character. God doesn't act on a whim. He waits for just the right time to do just the right thing. Is there any area of your life where you wish you had more self-control? God can help. Perhaps you need to lose weight, just say no to gossip, or keep your temper in check. Ask God for the desire and the discipline to wisely exercise restraint.

Lord, I need Your help in all those areas. Every day my tongue gets me in trouble: it wants to speak too much; it wants to eat too much. I pray that You would help me to hold my tongue unless I am speaking words of praise or encouragement. Amen.

Day 56

He Listens

"Then you will call upon Me and come and pray to Me, and I will listen to you."
JEREMIAH 29:12 NLV

This verse holds an amazing promise: the God of heaven and earth, the ruler of all kingdoms and powers, listens to me. If you've ever stood outside on a clear night under a glittering canopy of stars and felt insignificant, this verse assures us that we are anything but invisible to God. Just pray, and He will listen. And not only will He listen, but He'll help, comfort, and teach. He isn't merely a powerless, empathetic listening ear. He is the one who spoke life into existence. When you speak, He listens—and when He speaks, things change. Take your cares to Him today.

Lord, I feel small in this universe, but You see me even in the midst of the masses. You love me, and You can change my circumstances. Thank You. In Jesus' name, amen.

Day 57

Never in Conflict

He began to speak boldly in the synagogue, but when Priscilla and Aquila heard him, they took him aside and explained to him the way of God more accurately.
ACTS 18:26 ESV

Greet Prisca and Aquila, my fellow workers in Christ Jesus.
ROMANS 16:3 ESV

Our God-given gifts and abilities are to be used with knowledge of God's Word and in tandem with the life and family He has given us. The use of God's gifts never conflicts with the truth of His Word and is always in harmony with our surrender to His will.

The woman, Priscilla or Prisca, used her teaching skills alongside her husband and was commended by the apostle Paul. She models the concept of harmony of scripture and gift.

I need discernment, Lord, as a I seek to understand how You want me to use my gifts. Amen.

Day 58

Hearing from Jesus

Long ago God spoke many times and in many ways to our ancestors through the prophets. And now in these final days, he has spoken to us through his Son. God promised everything to the Son as an inheritance, and through the Son he created the universe.

HEBREWS 1:1–2 NLT

When you look at Jesus, you get a clear picture of God. And He can speak directly to you. You may not hear an out-loud voice, but Jesus can speak to your heart as He answers your prayers and talks to you. And He will make Himself clear to you if you seek Him. In Jeremiah 29:13 (NIV), God says, "You will seek me and find me when you seek me with all your heart." Ask Jesus to speak clearly to you today. What is He saying?

Jesus, Help me to be able to hear from You and get to know Your voice.

Day 59

No Turning Back

We are not of those people who turn back and are lost. Instead, we have faith to be saved from the punishment of sin. Now faith is being sure we will get what we hope for. It is being sure of what we cannot see.

HEBREWS 10:39–11:1 NLV

Keep your eye on the prize—it's good advice in competition and in Christianity. Our prize as followers of Christ may not be a higher-paying job, popularity, or the perfect life, but it's priceless nonetheless. Jesus chose us from the beginning of time to be the recipients of grace. He paid dearly to deliver us from a grave situation—the punishment of sin. Our faith assures us that our hope isn't misguided, that Jesus did indeed rise from the dead and deliver grace and eternal life to us.

Lord, I never want to turn back from following You. My faith tells me my hope in You is well placed. Amen.

Day 60

The Ultimate Bodyguard

Fear of the L*ORD leads to life, bringing security and protection from harm.*

PROVERBS 19:23 NLT

Fear sounds like a rather dubious route to take to find security. After all, you wouldn't hire a personal bodyguard you feared would harm you. But fearing God isn't the same as being afraid of Him. Fearing God means standing in awe of Him. After all, He's the almighty Creator, our sovereign master, the righteous judge of all. But this all-powerful God is *for* you. He's on your side, fighting on your behalf. Talk about the ultimate bodyguard!

If You are for us, Lord, who can be against us? Help us to remember these wonderful words of life when we start fearing things other than You. Nothing in this life—not death, not disease, not disaster—should overwhelm us. You are sovereign over everything. Amen.

Day 61

Spiritual Arsenal

Put on all the armor that God gives, so you can defend yourself against the devil's tricks.

EPHESIANS 6:11 CEV

A woman donning armor brings to mind images of Xena the Warrior Princess or Joan of Arc. But the armor God offers is neither fantasy nor outdated. It's a spiritual arsenal of offensive and defensive gear. It's comprised of weapons such as truth, righteousness, peace, and faith. There's a battle going on every day for your mind and heart. But there's no reason to be afraid. Through faith, God's given you everything you need to be victorious.

Lord, thank You for the reminder that my only offensive weapon is Your Word. Forgive me for treating it lightly, for pushing it aside in favor of more urgent (to my mind) things. Nothing is more urgent than preparing for the battle You tell me I am already in. Help me to take up my "sword" daily. Amen.

Day 62

Strength for the Weak

He gives strength to the weak. And He gives power to him who has little strength. Even very young men get tired and become weak and strong young men trip and fall. But they who wait upon the Lord will get new strength. They will rise up with wings like eagles. They will run and not get tired. They will walk and not become weak.

ISAIAH 40:29–31 NLV

Could you use a large helping of God's power in your life? Who couldn't? The Bible says that those who wait for the Lord—the people who pray—will gain new strength! God gives strength and power to people who feel like they don't have any. . .if we simply come to Him in prayer and wait expectantly. Waiting for the Lord in prayer means that you expect Him to show up and keep His promises. You look for Him and you put your hope in Him.

Thank You for giving us Your strength, God.

Day 63

Worthy of Reverence

It is the LORD your God you must follow,
and him you must revere. Keep his commands
and obey him; serve him and hold fast to him.
DEUTERONOMY 13:4 NIV

Reverence is not a word we often use in today's culture. The world, caught up in glorifying self, has lost all sense of deep respect for our all-powerful Creator God. And the cancel culture we find ourselves engulfed in has left a pretty irreverent bunch. Will you choose to know more of Him, to love and obey Him? Or will you choose to make a god out of money, position, or power? Come closer to Him, friend. When you see for yourself how amazing God is, your heart will gladly reverence and honor Him.

Lord my God, thank You for showing me how wonderful You are! I love You and want to serve You. Help me to do only what pleases You. Amen.

Day 64

Walk by Faith

Our life is lived by faith. We do not live by what we see in front of us.
2 CORINTHIANS 5:7 NLV

I like to plan, make lists, and do things in order. It makes me uncomfortable when I don't know what's going to happen next. Imagining the faith of Abraham leaves me in awe. God told Abraham to leave his father's house and go to a land that He would show him. Now, maybe some of us wouldn't mind leaving a few pesky relatives behind, but Abraham had no idea where he was going! And he didn't ask God for an itinerary. Instead, he packed up everything he owned and set off for a promised inheritance.

Father, sometimes I have no idea where we're going, but I want to trust like Abraham and keep taking the next step. Keep my eyes fixed on You so I'm not distracted by what I see in front of me. Amen.

Day 65

Do Something Besides Talk

And if they are on the list, they will learn to be lazy and will spend their time gossiping from house to house, meddling in other people's business and talking about things they shouldn't.

1 TIMOTHY 5:13 NLT

This is certainly not one of the happiest or most flattering verses in the Bible, but it is a needed admonition. We must make sure that we do not neglect to use our gifts and rather become socialites and busybodies. That can happen, even in the church!

God gives many of us families, which are to be our first priority after Him. Then He may give us occasion to use our educational investment and personal giftedness in ways outside the home. We must not, instead, become lazy and spend our productive time talking and socially interacting, which can lead to gossip and other unhealthy tendencies.

Lord, keep me from becoming a slacker and a talker. Amen.

Day 66

Don't Give Up

If a man does things to please the Holy Spirit,
he will have life that lasts forever. Do not let yourselves
get tired of doing good. If we do not give up,
we will get what is coming to us at the right time.
GALATIANS 6:8–9 NLV

Quitters give up because they've run out of their own strength. They have nothing left to give, so they give up in defeat. But followers of Jesus depend on His strength. And it never runs out. Remember that His power shines through in our weakness. Allow Him to be your strength. Invite Him to give you power through His Spirit who is alive in you. Keep coming back to God every day in prayer, trusting that He is going before you.

Lord, Thank You that I don't have to depend on my own strength. I'd much rather count on Yours instead.

Day 67

Secure and Immovable

I am sure that nothing can separate us from God's love—not life or death, not angels or spirits, not the present or the future.
ROMANS 8:38 CEV

You can feel secure in your relationship with God. God doesn't suffer from mood swings or bad hair days. He isn't swayed by popular opinion or influenced by what others have to say about you. God's love, His character, His gift of salvation, and every promise He's ever made to you stands firm, immovable. You can lean on Him in any and every circumstance, secure in the fact that He'll never let you down.

Dear Father, it is an immeasurable blessing to be loved in this way by You. I do not love like this. My love is fickle, forgetful, and frail. Forgive me. Help me to learn better how to love those around me by studying Your unfailing love. Spirit, love through me. Amen.

Day 68

Nothing More. . .or Less!

"Jesus. . . There is salvation in no one else! God has given no other name under heaven by which we must be saved."

ACTS 4:11–12 NLT

God created you to live forever with Him. But like every other person since the dawn of time, you turned away from God to live life on your own terms. Yet God didn't give up on you. He sent His Son to pay the heavy price of your rebellion, to sacrifice His life for yours. When you place your faith in Jesus, you accept this gift. Your salvation is complete. There's nothing more or less you can do to be saved.

Lord, this is a gift that You are—even now—extending to everyone. It's not an exclusive club; it's not for the rich or the poor, the beautiful or the very bad. It's for all who believe. Thank You for my salvation. Help me to tell others about it with joy. Amen.

Day 69

He Delivers

Faith is confidence in what we hope for
and assurance about what we do not see.
HEBREWS 11:1 NIV

It's been said that death and taxes are the only things we can be certain of in our lives. The Bible tells us that faith brings its own gift of certainty. Because of God's promises, and His faithfulness in keeping them in the past, we have the assurance that He'll come through for us in the future. He has promised we're loved, forgiven, cared for, and destined for heaven. Rest in the fact that what God promises, He delivers.

Lord, it is a miracle that, through faith, the unseen becomes more real and dear than what we can touch. We haven't seen You, yet we love You and believe in You with our whole heart. Thank You for that inexpressible joy. . .the certainty of our salvation. Amen.

Day 70

Worship, Woman!

O come, let us worship and bow down, let us kneel before the Lord our Maker [in reverent praise and supplication].
PSALM 95:6 AMPC

Worship is the compass of our lives. If we want to know what we value, let's look at what we worship. In the Old Testament, as He was establishing His people, Israel, God laid down very specific laws about idolatry, likening it to spiritual adultery, an earthly reference that was easily understood. He wanted them to know that as a loving husband desires his wife's devoted love, so He desired their hearts turned toward Him alone. These truths still apply to us today.

There is hope for a woman who worships the one true God. She may worship quietly, noisily, privately, or publicly, but her church is edified when others can observe it. And the condition of her heart is reflected in it.

Jehovah God, I worship You. Reveal to me any idols that threaten my love for You. Amen.

Day 71

Be Still

"Be still, and know that I am God! I will be honored by every nation. I will be honored throughout the world."
PSALM 46:10 NLT

Sometimes we need to be reminded that "God's got this." We wring our hands and suffer panic attacks from the uncertainty of living in this world, but all that anxious pacing is wasted energy. Our time is better spent in prayer than in panic. God gently shushes us like a mother to her upset child: "Rest easy. Just be still while I hold you. I'll take care of everything." As children we trust our parents completely to provide what we need and keep us safe, but as adults it's easier to strive than to trust. Today, rest in the knowledge that our God has big shoulders.

God, I give You my anxiety.
I trust You to work out Your plans. Amen.

Day 72

Never Stop Believing

Abraham never wavered in believing God's promise. In fact, his faith grew stronger, and in this he brought glory to God. He was fully convinced that God is able to do whatever he promises. And because of Abraham's faith, God counted him as righteous.

ROMANS 4:20–22 NLT

The Bible is filled with God's promises to us, His chosen children. The pages are lined with everything from our eternal home in heaven to everyday rest and peace in trusting Him. The key is to be like Abraham—never stop believing that God can and will do what He says. Abraham was fully convinced that although he and Sarah were physically beyond childbearing years, God would do the impossible and give them a son. And He did.

Father, I believe! I believe that You will make good on Your promises. Amen.

Day 73

Secret Ingredient

This is the secret: Christ lives in you.
This gives you assurance of sharing his glory.
COLOSSIANS 1:27 NLT

When it comes to family recipes, women often remain mum on the secret ingredient that makes their great-grandmother's pot roast, pound cake, or pickled beets stand out from the rest. You have a secret ingredient in your life that ensures your future will turn out perfectly. But this secret—that once you put your faith in Jesus, you are assured of spending eternity with Him—is meant for sharing. Pass it on, and you'll be blessing future generations!

Lord, we are the aroma of Christ to a starving world! We praise You for Your amazing grace. We have no aroma or flavor on our own that would attract anyone—but through You, we partake of that divine goodness and others are drawn in. Praise the Lord! Amen.

Day 74

Peace in the Midst of Problems

Let the peace of Christ rule in your hearts, since as members of one body you were called to peace. And be thankful.

Colossians 3:15 NIV

When you let peace have power over your heart, it means that you have an inner calm that comes from trusting Jesus. When problems come, and they will, you trust in Jesus and His power over anything. When you get in the daily habit of praying and taking all of your problems, worries, and concerns to Jesus, you begin to experience the kind of peace that Jesus offers. When you're dealing with stress or too many things that are going on at once, turn your focus off yourself and onto Jesus and others. Help someone else. Turn on the praise music. And thank God for His peace in your heart.

Lord, Help me to focus on You daily, to look at You and Your power instead of my problems.

Day 75

Proper Expression

Let the message about Christ, in all its richness, fill your lives. Teach and counsel each other with all the wisdom he gives. Sing psalms and hymns and spiritual songs to God with thankful hearts.

COLOSSIANS 3:16 NLT

The so-called "worship wars" have raged for a while in churches and will probably do so as long as there are people with differing opinions and ages and preferences. Sometimes there are valid points of reference, sometimes not. But in every situation, there are those who think a certain type of music is better suited for worship and Christian expression.

Be a woman of hope by remembering that the energy of the accompaniment or the coolness of the lyrics should never outshine the message of doctrine or redemption. Pray for your church's musical team.

Lord, guide those in music ministry at my church. Give them inspiration and wisdom. Amen.

Day 76

Found

Salvation is not a reward for the good things we have done, so none of us can boast about it.

EPHESIANS 2:9 NLT

You're lost at sea, drowning. There's no hope of saving yourself. Then members of the Coast Guard appear. They pull you from the frigid water—no questions asked. They don't save you because of your impressive résumé or because you're such a kind woman. They save you because you need saving. Jesus saved you because you took hold of His hand in faith when He offered to pull you from the waves. Without Him, you were lost. Now, you're found—saved and secure.

Dear Lord, we can never do enough good things or obey perfectly enough to deserve saving. Hallelujah! It is a free gift offered to us when we recognize that we desperately need to be saved. Thank You, Lord, for doing what we could never do for ourselves. Amen.

Day 77

Big Plans

"'For I know the plans I have for you,' says the Lord, 'plans for well-being and not for trouble, to give you a future and a hope.'"
JEREMIAH 29:11 NLV

Abraham thought God was trustworthy, and his belief was credited to his heavenly account as righteousness. God had epic plans for Abraham's offspring—saving-the-world kind of epic. And He hasn't neglected you, His chosen daughter, in His planning. Comparison is an easy trap to stumble into. We look around and wish we could be like someone else. From the outside, their life, family, or personality seem like a better option. But remember that if you're busy trying to be someone else, you're missing out on God's unique plans that only you can live.

Father, I trust that You have something special in store for my life, things You've positioned me to do. Keep my focus on You. Amen.

Day 78

Drawn Toward Jesus

Have the same mindset as Christ Jesus: who, being in very nature God, did not consider equality with God something to be used to his own advantage.

PHILIPPIANS 2:5–6 NIV

Even those who don't believe Jesus is God can agree that He was an extraordinary person. The way Jesus selflessly loved others, reaching out to people whom society had cast aside—including women—demonstrates an attitude of compassion, humility, and service. We're drawn to those who sincerely care for us. That's one reason why we're drawn toward Jesus. Believing in a God who believes in us doesn't feel risky; it feels like accepting a free invitation to be unconditionally loved.

Dear Lord, thank You for loving us so much that You would send Your only Son to die for our sins. Help us to be more like You to the people around us. Help us to love, to welcome, to serve. Help us to offer both truth and grace in Your precious Name. Amen.

Day 79

Fellowship and Food

And day after day they regularly assembled in the temple with united purpose, and in their homes they broke bread [including the Lord's Supper]. They partook of their food with gladness and simplicity and generous hearts.

Acts 2:46 AMPC

Who doesn't love a church potluck? Tables and tables of casseroles and mashed potatoes and sweet corn and rolls followed by tables of pies and cakes and gooey desserts of every sort. Ahh, the wonder of it!

It seems that the congregation of the early church had some kind of shared meals too. Of course, they would have the Lord's Supper as well as regular kinds of meals together. Right at the beginning, they realized as the Spirit led them that fellowship among believers is important.

Lord Jesus, You instituted the Lord's Supper and You enjoyed fellowship with Your friends in Bethany. We need to follow Your example. Amen.

Day 80

Belonging to God

But now the Lord Who made you, O Jacob, and He Who made you, O Israel, says, "Do not be afraid. For I have bought you and made you free. I have called you by name. You are Mine!"

ISAIAH 43:1 NLV

When you're feeling insecure, God wants you to remember something: no matter where you are, you are His! He knows your name, He is with you, and you never have to be afraid in new places or situations. When Jesus Himself tells you who you are, it changes everything. You are His beloved child. He paid the price for your freedom when He gave His life for you on the cross. You have direct access to the one who sees everything and knows everything. And you can be confident in every situation.

Lord, I'm so thankful that I belong to You. Help me to be confident in the truth that You are always with me.

Day 81

Safety Comes from the Lord

In peace I will both lie down and sleep;
for you alone, O Lord, make me dwell in safety.
Psalm 4:8 ESV

Safety in our communities is a precious commodity.

The psalmist David knew what it was to lie down to sleep in volatile situations: on the run from King Saul who was trying to kill him, in the palace of a pagan king, in hiding from one of his sons who was staging a coup in the kingdom. And no doubt, David had spent a few nights in the fields with his sheep. But in all these situations, safety comes from the Lord.

And so it is with us. Let's do whatever we can to bring the hope of the Lord to our communities.

Father in heaven, I ask You to guide me as I try to bring Your hope to my community. Amen.

Day 82

Lean In

Trust in the Lord with all your heart and lean not on your own understanding; in all your ways submit to him, and he will make your paths straight.

Proverbs 3:5–6 niv

Every time we board an airplane, stow our carry-on, and buckle into our seat, we trust that even if we don't understand the physics involved, the plane has been correctly designed to defy gravity and fly us to our destination. We trust the engineers who do understand all that complicated math. And yet too often we fail to trust in God's abilities. Today, when you find yourself unsure about what to do, lean into God. Ask Him what He wants you to do, and then do it. He promises to straighten out those winding paths if only you'll trust Him.

Father, teach me to trust You with my whole heart and to be obedient. Amen.

Day 83
Glorious Benefits

God sent Christ to be our sacrifice. Christ offered his life's blood, so that by faith in him we could come to God.
ROMANS 3:25 CEV

It's easy to focus solely on the glorious benefits of believing in God. Gifts like forgiveness, eternal life, a fresh start, and unconditional love are certainly worth celebrating. But each of these gifts comes at a very high cost. Jesus paid for them with His life. Jesus' sacrifice involved physical suffering, humiliation, betrayal, and separation from His Father. Choosing to follow Jesus will involve sacrifice on your part. Allow Him to show you how sacrifice can lead to something good.

Dear Lord, sometimes (or often, if we're being honest) we grumble about the suffering we are going through. Forgive us. Let us instead praise You for the suffering You allow us to experience. That is how, in Your inscrutable mercy, You are forming us into the likeness of Your Son. Amen.

Day 84

Ahead and Behind

For the L*ORD will go ahead of you; yes,*
the God of Israel will protect you from behind.
ISAIAH 52:12 NLT

Yes, our great God is striding ahead of us. He is before us and behind us and with us always. There are many scriptures to support this constant truth. Let this be our heartfelt prayer: "Train me, GOD, to walk straight; then I'll follow your true path. Put me together, one heart and mind; then, undivided, I'll worship in joyful fear. From the bottom of my heart I thank you, dear Lord; I've never kept secret what you're up to. You've always been great toward me—what love!" (Psalm 86:11–13 MSG).

Thank You, Lord, for all You've taught me and made known to me from Your Word. I choose not to live in fear because I know You are ahead of me, behind me, and alive inside of me.

Day 85

Faith That Won't Fail

If Christ wasn't raised to life, our message
is worthless, and so is your faith.
1 CORINTHIANS 15:14 CEV

Faith, in and of itself, is nothing more than trust. If you place your trust in something that isn't trustworthy, your faith is futile. You can have faith that money grows on trees, but ultimately, that faith isn't going to help you pay your bills. Putting your faith in Jesus is different. Historical and biblical eyewitness accounts back up Jesus' claims. That means putting your faith in Jesus is both logical and powerful. It's a faith that won't fail.

Lord, we thank You for being the God who both walked on mountains and moves them still. Thank You for being the God who spoke in the past and speaks even today. Thank You for being trustworthy and true. We place our hope in You—both now and in the future. Amen.

Day 86

God's Favorite Gift

"Obedience is better than sacrifice, and submission is better than offering the fat of rams."
1 Samuel 15:22 NLT

Suppose you had a daughter who broke every rule you made. She jumped on the furniture, hit her little brother, and swiped money from your wallet. Every day. But every evening, she offered you her dessert, telling you how much she loved you. The next day it was disobedience as usual. Have you ever been that little girl in God's eyes? Making sacrifices in God's name is commendable. But first, do what God asks. Obedience is God's favorite gift.

Dear Lord, often I don't see my own disobedience; I just see the noble sacrifices I have made in Your name. Lord, those sacrifices mean nothing if I expect them to cover my sins. Only Your blood can do that. Only Your Spirit can teach me obedience, amen.

Day 87

The Loving Choice

Pursue a righteous life—a life of wonder, faith, love, steadiness, courtesy. Run hard and fast in the faith.
1 TIMOTHY 6:11–12 MSG

Wearing white after Labor Day used to be considered taboo. But what was accepted as "right" in your mother's generation is not always considered "right" today. With God, the rules never change. What's right is always right. Living a righteous life means consistently choosing to do what's right in God's eyes. Doing what's right may not always be the popular choice, but it will always be the loving choice, the one God would make if He were in your shoes.

Lord, I am so swayed by other people's opinions, so afraid to be different or to stand out from the crowd. But I know the only opinion that really matters is Yours. Give me the strength to stand for the truth. Give me the courage to speak Your name to others. Amen.

Day 88

With All Your Heart

"You will look for Me and find Me,
when you look for Me with all your heart."
JEREMIAH 29:13 NLV

These words were penned to the surviving exiles in Babylon, people who probably felt abandoned by God after years in captivity. Sometimes we too lead ourselves into years of captivity to sin. We knowingly choose to do the wrong thing—gossip, addictions, lies, unforgiveness, and anger, and then we do it again and again. We walk right into the cell and slap the irons around our own wrists. And through our stubborn rebellion, God begins to feel distant. But there's hope for you, sweet friend. Just as He brought the Babylonian exiles home, He'll bring you home too. You'll find Him again if you search with your whole heart.

Father, I've been wrong. Please forgive me.
Show me the way back to You. Amen.

Day 89

Balance

Let the Spirit renew your thoughts and attitudes. Put on your new nature, created to be like God—truly righteous and holy.

EPHESIANS 4:23–24 NLT

Women are notorious for having moods that shift at the slightest provocation. We may blame it on hormones, stress, or the demands of those around us. Regardless of what pushes our mood swings to an all-time high, the truth is we all need an attitude adjustment now and then. Faith provides exactly what we require. As we turn to God in prayer, His Spirit makes us more like Him. He balances our lives and emotions with His power and perspective.

Dear Father, I desperately need Your renewal today. Forgive me for how I have lashed out at those around me; forgive me for how I have forgotten to put on the mind of Christ. Thank You for Your Spirit, pointing out my weaknesses and reminding me of Christ's sufficiency. Amen.

Day 90

Praying for Your Street

Whoever pursues righteousness and kindness
will find life, righteousness, and honor.
PROVERBS 21:21 ESV

Morality in our communities goes beyond meetings by the town council or homeowners association; morality is also determined by what happens in the homes along the streets.

On almost every street in every community in every town across the nation, there is immorality. Sexual sin has slithered into our neighborhoods and destroyed our marriages and families—and even our understanding of gender and the value of life. Being a woman of hope in your community means praying for the homes along your street and asking God to bring the light of righteousness.

Holy God, I pray that You would put a desire in my neighbors' hearts to pursue righteous lives. In Jesus' name. Amen.

Day 91

Wiped Away

God, in his grace, freely makes us right in his sight. He did this through Christ Jesus when he freed us from the penalty for our sins.
ROMANS 3:24 NLT

Saying you're righteous is the same as saying you're blameless. And that's what God says about you. Once you put your faith and trust in Jesus, every trace of your past rebellion against God is wiped away. It's as though you lived Jesus' life, morally perfect and wholly good. What's more, this righteousness covers your future as well as your past. Anytime you stumble, go straight to God. Confess what you've done. You can trust it's forgiven *and* forgotten.

Dear Father, we praise You for Your undeserved kindness to us and our undeserved righteousness through Jesus Christ. There is nothing we can say except thank You. There is nothing we can do except praise You for the forgiveness that covers our past and extends into our future. Amen.

Day 92

Love Letter

He will have much joy over you. With His love He will give you new life. He will have joy over you with loud singing.
ZEPHANIAH 3:17 NLV

Oh, the sweet anticipation of reading the words of someone who loves you! Likely you keep them in a special place and read them over and over. We all want to feel cherished, to know someone cares, looks forward to seeing us, and thinks about us. How would you feel if God wrote you a love letter telling you how delighted He is with you? He did! The Bible is the story of His great love for you. You're special to Him, and He thinks about you all the time. Open your Bible and consider that God wants you to know Him as intimately as He knows you.

Heavenly Father, Your love for me is unmatched. I want to know You more. Amen.

Day 93

God with Us

"The virgin will conceive and give birth to a son, and they will call him Immanuel" (which means "God with us").

MATTHEW 1:23 NIV

Jesus is Immanuel. This special name was foretold back in the Old Testament in the book of Isaiah, hundreds of years before Jesus was born (see Isaiah 7:14). God had a rescue plan in place for His people. John 3:16–17 (NIV) tells us why: "For God so loved the world that he gave his one and only Son, that whoever believes in him shall not perish but have eternal life. For God did not send his Son into the world to condemn the world, but to save the world through him."

God became one of us. Immanuel. He is with you always.

Jesus, I'm amazed that You became one of us. Thank You for Your unimaginable sacrifice for me.

Day 94

The End of Myself

Just then a woman who had been sick with a flow of blood for twelve years came from behind. She touched the bottom of His coat. She said to herself, "If I only touch the bottom of His coat, I will be healed." Then Jesus turned around. He saw her and said, "Daughter, take hope! Your faith has healed you." At once the woman was healed.

MATTHEW 9:20–22 NLV

As every option was exhausted for this woman, hopelessness probably took root. But then she heard about Jesus. And she believed He was the long-awaited Messiah, the Son of God, who had the power to change what she could not, so she reached out for the hem of His garment. And Jesus knew, as He always does. When you reach the end of yourself, reach out to Him.

Father, I know You have the power to change hard circumstances. Help me to turn to You first. Amen.

Day 95

Heart Changes

Jesus went to Galilee preaching the Message of God: "Time's up! God's kingdom is here. Change your life and believe the Message."

MARK 1:14–15 MSG

What you believe will influence the choices you make. If you believe in gravity, you won't jump from a seventh-story balcony to save time in getting to your hair appointment. If you believe what Jesus says, you'll change the way you live. Jesus often talks about the importance of traits such as honesty, purity, and generosity. Though God's Spirit helps change your heart, it's the daily choices you make that help bring traits like these to maturity.

Lord, help me to trust that my obedience is bearing fruit even when it feels like nothing is really changing. Help me to keep believing that You are working in and through me. Help me to see—without knowing the ending—that You are writing my story. Amen.

Day 96

Care for the Needy

"For I was hungry and you gave me food, I was thirsty and you gave me drink, I was a stranger and you welcomed me, I was naked and you clothed me, I was sick and you visited me, I was in prison and you came to me."

MATTHEW 25:35–36 ESV

With our advanced medical knowledge, life expectancy is longer than it was a century or so ago. And that means that many will become caregivers to their aging parents or other relatives.

Jesus told His listeners that whenever we provide care for someone who is needy, we are actually doing a service to Him. We have not usually thought of this verse in reference to caregivers, but it does seem to apply. Pray for the caregivers in your community; they need it.

Dear Lord, bless those in my community who are sitting with a loved one today. In Jesus' name, amen.

Day 97

He Is with Me

There is one body [of believers] and one Spirit—just as you were called to one hope when called [to salvation]—one Lord, one faith, one baptism, one God and Father of us all who is [sovereign] over all and [working] through all and [living] in all.

EPHESIANS 4:4–6 AMP

Repeat this to yourself: "He is with me. He is with me. He is with me."

The God of heaven is with you. Do you trust Him? Is there anything in your heart and mind right now that is having trouble with this truth? Ask Jesus to make that known to you. He wants you to live your life in victorious freedom. Even when you're facing hard times, and even when you've been scarred by betrayal and devastation, He is with you. He is going before you. He wants to heal your hurts.

Jesus, I want to believe that You are at work in me. Please make Yourself known to me.

Day 98

Held Together

He is before all things, and in him all things hold together.
COLOSSIANS 1:17 NIV

Jesus is more powerful than anything you can imagine, and yet He loves and cares for you. He knows everything about you, and He cares about the things you're going through. Sometimes that can be hard to believe, but the Bible tells us it is true. And Jesus will show up and be very real in your life if you let Him. Are you facing a problem that feels too big or too small for God? Talk to Him about it. Tell Him how you really feel. Ask Him to help you believe that He cares about every little thing—and every big thing too. The closer you get to Jesus, the more your thoughts begin to match up with His thoughts.

Lord, I'm amazed that You truly care so much for me. Thank You for holding me together.

Day 99

Help for the Disquiet

Why are you cast down, O my inner self? And why should you moan over me and be disquieted within me? Hope in God and wait expectantly for Him, for I shall yet praise Him, Who is the help of my countenance, and my God.

PSALM 42:11 AMPC

Anxiety disorders have been around since ancient times. In the Bible, we find that many of the emotions we face have been addressed by the inspired writers.

Anxiety causes a disquiet in the inner self. It makes the thoughts swirl and the brain seem noisy with confusion. It is difficult to focus and challenging to believe what others say.

The psalmist points to the Lord as the Help for which we can wait expectantly. He is trustworthy.

Heavenly Father, I look to You for the calm I cannot bring to myself. I wait on You. Amen.

Day 100

Safe House

God's a safe-house for the battered, a sanctuary during bad times. The moment you arrive, you relax; you're never sorry you knocked.

PSALM 9:9–10 MSG

Have you ever gone through bad times? Maybe you're feeling battered by life right now—as if you were chosen only to struggle and never to thrive. Friend, whether it's an illness, a wayward child, financial struggles, or anxiety, you can find hope, help, and shelter in your heavenly Father. As the scripture says, the moment you arrive in His presence, you'll relax. He may not remove all your problems, but He'll change and strengthen you through them. Go to Him in prayer. Find Him in His Word. Trust Him, and He will never forsake you.

Father, I need a place of shelter, a safe place to rest my anxiety-burdened mind. I'm chosen to thrive in this dry place. Amen.

Day 101

The Only Way

Jesus said, "I am the Way and the Truth and the Life. No one can go to the Father except by Me."
JOHN 14:6 NLV

Jesus is the only true God. Acts 4:12 (NIV) tells us, "Salvation is found in no one else, for there is no other name under heaven given to mankind by which we must be saved." Jesus is all the fullness of God in human form (Colossians 2:9), and He is the image of the invisible God (Colossians 1:15). Jesus is how we can see God (John 1:18). God Himself came down to find you through Jesus. He is the Way, the Truth, and the Life.

Jesus, I believe that You are the one true God. I will follow You because You are the only way and the truth.

Day 102

Life Letter

These are written so that you will put your faith in Jesus as the Messiah and the Son of God. If you have faith in him, you will have true life.

JOHN 20:31 CEV

The Bible is like a letter from your best friend. In it, God shares how much He loves you, what He's been up to since the creation of the world, and His plans for the future. You're an important part of those plans. The life you live through faith is the letter you write in return. But others will also sneak a peek at your "life letter." The life you live may be the only Bible some people ever read.

Lord, I want my life to be a living representation of the gospel—to live with visible repentance and joy. But often I shudder at speaking the truth. Help me to be discontent with simply showing; help me to tell. For how will others know if they have not heard? Amen.

Day 103

Get Rid of Pride

God sets Himself against the proud (the insolent, the overbearing, the disdainful, the presumptuous, the boastful)—[and He opposes, frustrates, and defeats them], but gives grace (favor, blessing) to the humble.

1 PETER 5:5 AMPC

Pride is an ugly sin. It was the sin of Lucifer, the brightest angel of heaven, who fell and became the archenemy of the God who created him. It was the sin of Eve, who lusted for more than God had given, thinking she deserved more and instead lost what she did have when she sinned.

Pride causes us to do ugly things and feel ugly ways. God hates pride. But He gives grace to those who are humble. If you struggle with feelings of pride, make a deliberate choice to humble yourself and ask for God's help to surrender it.

Father God, reveal to me any pride in my heart and give me the grace to deal with it. Amen.

Day 104

History

"And he made from one man every nation of mankind to live on all the face of the earth, having determined allotted periods and the boundaries of their dwelling place, that they should seek God, and perhaps feel their way toward him and find him. Yet he is actually not far from each one of us, for 'In him we live and move and have our being.'"

ACTS 17:26–28 ESV

God knows your name and everything about you. He set you on earth at this exact time in history for a purpose. He wants you to know Him. He wants you to love Him and love others through Him. You matter greatly to God, and He has wonderful plans for your life.

Lord, I'm coming to believe the truth of Your great love for me personally. I want what You want for my life. Thank You for placing me at this spot in Your great story.

Day 105

Cure Your Worry

Don't worry about anything; instead, pray about everything. Tell God what you need, and thank him for all he has done. Then you will experience God's peace, which exceeds anything we can understand. His peace will guard your hearts and minds as you live in Christ Jesus.

PHILIPPIANS 4:6–7 NLT

A moment's peace is priceless, but what if that moment stretched to a lifetime? Philippians maps out God's perfect plan for everlasting peace of mind. In short, don't worry. Saturate your day with prayer instead. Pour out your worries, frustrations, fears, and even your anger to the God who will always listen. He can handle all your jumbled feelings—after all, He created emotions. And have faith that God is in control. Thank Him for His tender care. Then an indescribable peace will flow into your life.

Father, thank You so much for replacing my worry with peace when I trust You. Amen.

Day 106

Everything Is Possible

Jesus looked at them intently and said, "Humanly speaking, it is impossible. But with God everything is possible."
MATTHEW 19:26 NLT

What Jesus wants one person to do is not necessarily the same exact thing He wants you to do. Jesus is all about relationship. He is a very personal God. He wants to be your friend and your trusted counselor. He wants you to come to Him first for advice. What do you need advice about today? Ask Jesus for help and guidance. Talk to Him like you would talk to your best friend. You can talk to Him out loud, or you can pray in your heart and mind. And writing down your prayers so you can have a reminder of how God answers is also very helpful.

God, I believe that everything is possible with You leading me. I trust You to equip me for whatever You're calling me to do.

Day 107

When God Helps

The LORD is my strength and shield. I trust him with all my heart. He helps me, and my heart is filled with joy. I burst out in songs of thanksgiving. . . . Lead [your people] like a shepherd, and carry them in your arms forever.

PSALM 28:7, 9 NLT

When God helps, He turns darkness and stress and sadness into joy and singing and thanksgiving! It's always a process. God values you, and He is careful with you. He leads you like a gentle shepherd carries his sheep. When you allow Him to help you work through your issues and feelings, miraculous things happen. He knows exactly what you need and how to get you from one step to the next. Picture yourself being carried in the arms of Jesus. What truth does He want you to remember forever?

Thank You for being gentle with me, Lord Jesus.

Day 108

One Spirit

But the person who is joined to the Lord is one spirit with him.
1 CORINTHIANS 6:17 NLT

Let these scriptures encourage you today:

> Yet for us there is but one God, the Father, who is the source of all things, and we exist for Him; and one Lord, Jesus Christ, by whom are all things [that have been created], and we [believers exist and have life and have been redeemed] through Him. (1 Corinthians 8:6 AMP)
>
> God is faithful [He is reliable, trustworthy and ever true to His promise—He can be depended on], and through Him you were called into fellowship with His Son, Jesus Christ our Lord. (1 Corinthians 1:9 AMP)

Lord, You are faithful, reliable, trustworthy, and true to Your promise. I know I can depend on You always. I'm thankful that Your Spirit is in me and that You've filled me with new life.

Day 109

The Good Shepherd

I am the Good Shepherd.
The Good Shepherd gives His life for the sheep.
JOHN 10:11 NLV

Jesus tells us that He is our Shepherd. A good and gentle shepherd would love and care for his sheep with compassion and kindness. A shepherd needed the sheep to listen to him so they could travel to the best places for food. When the shepherd walked ahead of them, they followed him because they knew his voice. Jesus calls us His sheep, and He lovingly cares for each of us! Today's verse reminds us that our Shepherd even gave His very life for us! When we get to know His voice, we can be sure we're following someone we can trust.

Jesus, You are my loving Shepherd. I follow You because I trust You and know that I can count on You to lead me in the right direction.

Day 110
We Are His Sheep

When he saw the crowds, he had compassion on them because they were confused and helpless, like sheep without a shepherd.
MATTHEW 9:36 NLT

Sheep are born with an instinct to follow the leader. If one sheep does something dangerous or stupid, the sheep behind it usually follow. When Jesus came to earth, He saw that the people were acting like sheep without a shepherd—making bad choices and following others who were also making bad choices. Some people look at people making bad decisions and have no compassion for them. They judge them harshly and leave them to their consequences. But not Jesus. The Bible says that He had compassion on these people. He knew what caused them to make those choices. He loved them and wanted to help.

Jesus, thank You for leading me. Help me to be the kind of leader that has compassion and love for others.

Day 111

He Brings Out Your Best

God helping you: Take your everyday, ordinary life—
your sleeping, eating, going-to-work, and walking-around life—
and place it before God as an offering. Embracing what God
does for you is the best thing you can do for him. Don't become
so well-adjusted to your culture that you fit into it without even
thinking. Instead, fix your attention on God. You'll be changed
from the inside out. Readily recognize what he wants from
you, and quickly respond to it. Unlike the culture around you,
always dragging you down to its level of immaturity, God brings
the best out of you, develops well-formed maturity in you.

ROMANS 12:1–2 MSG

You were chosen to stand out from the crowd. Just like the shocked little New Testament boy, God can feed five thousand with your two fish, be they time, money, skills, or even just a meal for your neighbor.

God, bring out the best potential You see in me. Amen.

Day 112

Into Practice

Truth, righteousness, peace, faith, and salvation are more than words. Learn how to apply them. You'll need them throughout your life. God's Word is an indispensable weapon.

EPHESIANS 6:14–17 MSG

What you do with God's words is ultimately what you decide to do with God. If you read the Bible for inspiration, without application, your faith will never be more than a heartwarming pastime. While it's true that the Bible can be a source of comfort, it's also a source of power and an instrument of change. Invite God's Spirit to sear the Bible's words into your heart. Then step out in faith and put what you've learned into practice.

Dear Lord, we want to be doers of the Word, not hearers only. But so often we are content with a lukewarm, passive faith that shies away from engagement. Forgive us, and show us how Your Spirit working in us can turn truth, righteousness, peace, faith, and salvation into actions. Amen.

Day 113

Prayer Life

He is not weak or ineffective in dealing with you, but powerful within you. For even though He was crucified in weakness [yielding Himself], yet He lives [resurrected] by the power of God [His Father]. For we too are weak in Him [as He was humanly weak], yet we are alive and well [in fellowship] with Him because of the power of God directed toward you.

2 CORINTHIANS 13:3–4 AMP

We can have a deep and meaningful prayer life because of this truth. Prayer is about relationship. Talk to God now in your heart or out loud and wait for His response. Sometimes He will point you to a scripture. Sometimes He will put a picture in your imagination. He might put a worship song in your mind. He may impress your heart with a strong idea or thought. Our Creator can speak to us in unlimited ways.

God, I believe in Your unlimited power directed toward me. I want to hear from You in any way You want to speak.

Day 114

Clean Me Up

Create in me a clean heart, O God. Renew a loyal spirit within me. Do not banish me from your presence, and don't take your Holy Spirit from me. Restore to me the joy of your salvation, and make me willing to obey you.

PSALM 51:10–12 NLT

The Bible says David was a man after God's own heart, chosen by Him to slay giants and reign over a nation as king. Chosen, just as you are, for God's purpose. But David wasn't perfect, and neither are we. This psalm gives hope to all who've ever messed up. David wrote this psalm from a place of desolate brokenness. He begged God not to cast him aside because of his sin but to restore his joy and willingness to do what's right.

Father, I've sinned against You. But I know that if I confess, You are faithful to forgive. Bring back my joy. Amen.

Day 115

Our Safe Place

God is our safe place and our strength. He is always our help when we are in trouble. So we will not be afraid, even if the earth is shaken and the mountains fall into the center of the sea.

PSALM 46:1–2 NLV

The Bible tells us that God is our safe place. People, relationships, and circumstances change, but your safe place in God will never change. You can always count on Him to be the same. And you never have to be afraid when He is close. He wants to protect you, comfort you, and tell you how loved you are. Sometimes sitting in the quiet with God is the best way to pray. Ask Him to fill you with His love as you sit in His presence. Picture yourself climbing into God's lap and letting Him love you.

Thanks for always being a safe place for me, Father God!

Day 116

The Exchange Line

To bestow on them a crown of beauty instead of ashes, the oil of joy instead of mourning, and a garment of praise instead of a spirit of despair.

Isaiah 61:3 NIV

Remember the last time you were in the exchange line? That's never fun. Did you know that God likes to exchange things? Old for new, death for life, ashes for beauty, sadness for joy, despair for praise. He also exchanges our weakness for His strength. Can you picture yourself bringing everything that you need Him to exchange and laying it at Jesus' feet? What does He want to give you instead? Ask Him!

God, I'm so thankful that You can turn my darkness into light, my sadness into joy, my ashes into beauty, and my weakness into Your strength. Please show me what You'd like to exchange in my life.

Day 117

Believing without Seeing

Jesus said, "So, you believe because you've seen with your own eyes. Even better blessings are in store for those who believe without seeing."

JOHN 20:29 MSG

If you're searching for a pair of shoes, you don't rely on a salesperson's description. You want to see them. Try them on. Walk around in them awhile. The same is true when it comes to trying on faith for size. We long to see the one we've chosen to place our faith in. But Jesus says believing without seeing holds its own special reward. Ask Jesus to help you better understand those blessings as you walk in faith today.

Lord, we know we won't really "see" until we see You face-to-face. The waiting is hard sometimes; our eyes strain to see through this dim glass. But we praise You that our faith grows in the waiting and that You are becoming more real, true, and beautiful to us all the time. Amen.

Day 118

Honesty

I pray to you, O Lord, my rock. Do not turn a deaf ear to me. For if you are silent, I might as well give up and die. Listen to my prayer for mercy as I cry out to you for help, as I lift my hands toward your holy sanctuary.

Psalm 28:1–2 NLT

You can be totally honest with God. You can't hide anything from Him anyway. Notice that the Psalms are full of brutal honesty. God is the safest place for you to share everything. He can shine His light on all your thoughts and feelings and help you work them out. Ask God to bring anything to light that needs to be discussed and worked through.

God, I am thankful that You are a safe place.
Cast away my fears. I want to be totally honest with You.
Help me to long for You and desire to be with You every day.

Day 119

Straight from God

God, the one and only—I'll wait as long as he says.
Everything I hope for comes from him, so why not?
PSALM 62:5 MSG

As His Word promises, God is a safe place to be and you can trust Him absolutely. Thank Him for being a safe refuge for you. When you mess up and when you succeed, God is safe. He delights in You. He shares your sorrows and your joys. Allow Him to be with you in those times. Bring your successes and failures to Jesus now, and let Him love you in them. Read all of Psalm 62 in *The Message* as your prayer today.

Lord God, I believe it's true that everything I hope for comes from You. You have the answers I'm looking for. You are the source of strength that I'm needing. I bring You my successes and my failures. I don't have to perform for You. You love me no matter what.

Day 120

Anytime

Now that we know what we have—Jesus, this great High Priest with ready access to God—let's not let it slip through our fingers. . . . So let's walk right up to him and get what he is so ready to give. Take the mercy, accept the help.

Hebrews 4:16–18 msg

You've likely seen the movies where the common people need special permission to come into the palace and see the king or queen. They bow low before the throne and use titles of honor to show respect. Of course God will always deserve our respect, but we don't need special permission to go into His presence anymore! Because of Jesus, you have the ability to walk right up to God and talk to Him any time of the day. You don't have to cower in fear! Jesus has made everything right for you before God.

Father God, thank You for always receiving me.

Day 121

No One Like You

There is no one like You among the gods, O Lord. And there are no works like Yours. All the nations You have made will come and worship before You, O Lord. And they will bring honor to Your name. For You are great and do great things. You alone are God.

Psalm 86:8–10 NLV

The time you spend with God will accomplish more than anything else you could ever do. Jeremiah 32:17 (ESV) says, "Ah, Lord God! It is you who have made the heavens and the earth by your great power and by your outstretched arm! Nothing is too hard for you." Ask God to help you believe that He can do anything. No problem is too hard, too big, or too small for God's help.

God of all creation, there is no one like You. I am so blessed to be able to bring everything on my heart to You in prayer and know that You want to help!

Day 122

Wait for It

But those who trust in the LORD will find new strength. They will soar high on wings like eagles. They will run and not grow weary. They will walk and not faint.

ISAIAH 40:31 NLT

God has chosen you as His daughter to run *your* race. Sometimes our packed schedules can make us feel important, and we derive our sense of worth from our busyness instead of from our identity as a child of God. But if we have no white space on our page, not only can we begin to feel wrung out, there's also very little room for God to write His story on our lives. Leave some margin in your time, wait for God's direction, and He promises the hope of endurance.

Father, You haven't called me to do everything, but You have called me to do something. Teach me to wait so You can make me soar. Amen.

Day 123

"Nowhere" Blessings

"Turn to face God so he can wipe away your sins, pour out showers of blessing to refresh you, and send you the Messiah he prepared for you, namely, Jesus."

ACTS 3:19–20 MSG

Blessings are gifts straight from God's hand. Some of them are tangible, like the gift of a chance acquaintance leading to a job offer that winds up helping to pay the bills. Some are less concrete. They may come wrapped in things like faith, joy, clarity, and contentment appearing seemingly out of "nowhere" amid difficult circumstances. The more frequently you thank God for His blessings, the more aware you'll be of how many more there are to thank Him for.

Dear Lord, help me to continually turn toward You. Your Word says that when I do, You will wipe away my sins and pour out showers of blessings to refresh me. Thank You for enabling me to turn back to You, over and over again. Amen.

Day 124

Power and Purpose

He delivered us and saved us and called us with a holy calling [a calling that leads to a consecrated life—a life set apart—a life of purpose], not because of our works [or because of any personal merit—we could do nothing to earn this], but because of His own purpose and grace [His amazing, undeserved favor] which was granted to us in Christ Jesus before the world began [eternal ages ago].

2 TIMOTHY 1:9 AMP

Jesus saves us and delivers us from our fears so that we can live a life of purpose. Ask Jesus to make His purpose for you clear. What are your gifts and talents? What stirs your heart in life-giving ways? Pray and listen as God writes this purpose on your heart. Make sure you write down any answer God is giving you. He will always confirm His truth for you if you ask Him.

Jesus, I'm so thankful that You want to replace my fears and anxieties with Your power and purpose.

Day 125

Ask and Receive

"So I say to you: Ask and it will be given to you; seek and you will find; knock and the door will be opened to you. For everyone who asks receives; the one who seeks finds; and to the one who knocks, the door will be opened."

LUKE 11:9–10 NIV

James 4:2 (NIV) says, "You do not have because you do not ask God." A lot of times we forget to bring things to God first. We try to get our needs met from other people and other things when God is just waiting for us to come to Him. We can ask for anything. And as we come to Him in prayer, He aligns our hearts with His.

Lord, please help me to come to You first with all my wants and needs. I know You want to help.

Day 126

Hope for the Hard Days

"If only my words were written! If only they were written down in a book! If only they were cut forever into the rock with an iron cutter and lead! But as for me, I know that the One Who bought me and made me free from sin lives, and that He will stand upon the earth in the end. Even after my skin is destroyed, yet in my flesh I will see God."

JOB 19:23–26 NLV

When you're slogging through a tough time, remember Job. We've all had bad days, but probably not like Job. God gave Satan permission to test Job, and the enemy set out to crush him. Job lost everything—possessions, children, health—but Satan couldn't touch his most precious possession, his faith in God. Job knew that no matter what atrocities happen in this life, our Redeemer lives, and one day we will see God.

Father, give me unwavering faith and hope like Job that looks ahead to the day I'll see You. Amen.

Day 127

Unlimited Power

And [so that you will begin to know] what the immeasurable and unlimited and surpassing greatness of His [active, spiritual] power is in us who believe.

EPHESIANS 1:19 AMP

The power of God is unlimited! Do you really believe that this truth applies to His power in your own life? Ask God to write this truth on your heart. It's a prayer He loves to answer. If you are struggling with doubt, bring that to Jesus. Ask Him if there are any lies you might be believing that could be preventing you from accepting the truth of His limitless power in your life.

Jesus, I believe You are all powerful. You are beyond my understanding and fully capable of taking care of everything I need. I ask that You erase any lies the enemy has been writing on my heart and fill me with Your truth. I want to trust You more. Continue to be real to me.

Day 128

Look and Find

"You will seek me and find me when you seek me with all your heart."
JEREMIAH 29:13 NIV

What does seeking God and looking for Him with all your heart mean? Check out the following verses that help us understand:

- I love those who love me, and those who seek me diligently find me. (Proverbs 8:17 ESV)
- "But seek first the kingdom of God and his righteousness, and all these things will be added to you." (Matthew 6:33 ESV)
- Seek the LORD and his strength; seek his presence continually! (1 Chronicles 16:11 ESV)
- Come near to God and he will come near to you. (James 4:8 NIV)

As you look for God in everything, you will find that He is everywhere. He never leaves you.

Thank You for being close to me, Lord. Help me to look for You in everything.

Day 129

Always Knocking

"Look! I stand at the door and knock. If you hear my voice and open the door, I will come in, and we will share a meal together as friends."
REVELATION 3:20 NLT

The Bible tells us we can knock on God's door and be invited in, but did you know that He is knocking on your door too? Today's scripture tells us this truth. Wouldn't the game of hide-and-seek be so easy if the person who was supposed to be hiding was actually looking for you too? That's the really amazing thing: while we're looking for God, He's looking for us! He wants you to find Him. He makes it pretty simple. If you look for Him, you will find Him. That's a promise!

Jesus, I'm so thankful that You don't play games. You want to be found. Help me to seek You always.

Day 130

Personal Trainer

Give your burdens to the Lord, and he will take care of you. He will not permit the godly to slip and fall.
Psalm 55:22 NLT

It's important for us women to do some heavy lifting as we age. Weight-bearing exercise helps keep our bones strong and our muscles toned. But bearing mental and emotional weight is another story. These don't build us up. They break us down. Allow faith to become your personal trainer when it comes to what's weighing heavily on your mind and heart. God knows how much weight you can bear. Invite Him to carry what you cannot.

Dear Father, You know the weights of worry, care, trouble, and trial that I cannot carry on my own; and You know how often I try to take those burdens out of Your loving hands. Help me to place them in Your arms over and over again, where they belong. Amen.

Day 131

Hearing from God

"My sheep listen to my voice; I know them, and they follow me."
JOHN 10:27 NLT

Have you limited the way God is "permitted" to speak to you? Consider the ways that you are comfortable hearing from God: through His Word, through a pastor, through music, through nature? Jesus respects our boundaries. If you've put boundaries, limits, and walls between you and God and what He is "allowed" to do in your life, your prayer life could be suffering. Ask God to break down and break through any walls you have built that might be creating a feeling of distance between you and God. Ask God to show Himself to you in new ways. Be open to the work of the Holy Spirit in your heart.

---

*I don't want to put limits on You, Lord.
Break down any walls that I've created that
might prevent me from hearing from You.*

Day 132

Prayer Life

Very early in the morning, while it was still dark, Jesus got up, left the house and went off to a solitary place, where he prayed.
MARK 1:35 NIV

The Bible says that Jesus often went away to be alone with God and pray. Hopefully, you are beginning to understand how much you matter to God and why it's important to spend time with Him. As a follower of Jesus, your power and hope and strength to make it through each day come from your time spent with God. Jesus lived a life of prayer. How can you live a life of prayer too? You invite Him into every moment of your day. You seek His thoughts when you need help. You ask for Him to give you love for others as you see people during the day.

Jesus, I invite You into every moment of my day. Remind me that You are with me at all times.

Day 133

Blessing

Jabez cried out to the God of Israel, saying, "Oh that You would indeed bless me and enlarge my border [property], and that Your hand would be with me, and You would keep me from evil so that it does not hurt me!" And God granted his request.

1 CHRONICLES 4:10 AMP

Jabez asked for God's blessing. And God gave it to Him! Asking for God's blessing is something we see throughout the entire Bible. Does this mean that God will always give us everything we ask for? No, because God always sees all and knows all. Something that we think might be good for us could actually turn out pretty bad. That's why we trust God's will. Asking for God's blessing is asking for His purpose and power in your life rather than asking Him to give you everything you want. God knows best.

Lord, I trust You to bless me in whatever way You choose.

Day 134

Worries into Prayers

Don't fret or worry. Instead of worrying, pray.
Let petitions and praises shape your worries into
prayers, letting God know your concerns.
PHILIPPIANS 4:6 MSG

Sometimes it feels like it's a woman's job to worry. If you can't be assured that all of your loved ones' physical and emotional needs are being met, fretting about them makes you feel involved—like you're loving them, even if you're powerless to help. But you know Someone who *does* have the power to help. Anytime you feel the weight of worry, whether it's over someone else's problems or your own, let faith relieve you of the burden. Turn your worries into prayers.

Dear God, it is not my nature to turn my worries into prayers, but I thank You that Your Spirit working in me gives me a new nature—one that can lift my worries up to You as many times as they raise their heads. Thank You for listening to my concerns. Amen.

Day 135

Bring Your Plans to Jesus

In all your ways know and acknowledge and recognize Him, and He will make your paths straight and smooth [removing obstacles that block your way].

PROVERBS 3:6 AMP

Decision-making is not as difficult as we make it. When we forget that God wants to help us make choices, we get confused and anxious. When we leave God out of the decision-making process, we face lots of unnecessary problems. Confess this truth to God in prayer. Ask forgiveness for the times you've left God out of the equation. Repent and ask God to help transform your thinking in this area. Listen for His voice as you go about your day, and He'll be with you, leading you in the right direction.

Lord, I trust that You care about everything I have on my schedule. I invite You to be a part of every plan and every decision. Remind me that You're here when I start to forget You.

Day 136

Chosen to Be United

"May they all be as one, Father, as You are in Me and I am in You. May they belong to Us. Then the world will believe that You sent Me."

JOHN 17:21 NLV

Getting along can be hard. Sometimes our feelings get hurt or we're busy and don't want to be bothered by the burdens of others. But Jesus' prayer for all believers was that they would belong to Him and to one another, united as one force. This unity is one of our strongest witnesses to a dark world where it's everyone for himself. They see believers come together with supernatural unity and know that something otherworldly is happening. They begin to believe that Jesus is the Son of the Most High.

Father, help me to get along with my faith family, to overlook offenses, and to take the time to understand the problems and setbacks others are struggling under. Amen.

Day 137

A Lavish Love

"I've loved you the way my Father has loved me. Make yourselves at home in my love. If you keep my commands, you'll remain intimately at home in my love."

JOHN 15:9 MSG

Knowing that the God of the universe knows us personally and loves us lavishly brings us great joy. The definition of *lavish* is "to give without limit." First John 3:1 (NIV) says, "See what great love the Father has lavished on us, that we should be called children of God! And that is what we are!" God loves you without limit. Nothing can change that. You don't deserve it, so you can't possibly earn it. Rest in that truth.

Father, Your lavish love is astounding. I can't begin to understand how You can know everything about me and still love me without limit! I don't deserve Your love, but I'm thankful. I love You, Lord God.

Day 138

Hope for a City

And I saw the holy city, new Jerusalem, coming down out of heaven from God, prepared as a bride adorned for her husband.

Revelation 21:2 ESV

There are country-dwelling folks down here who wouldn't live in a city for any amount of money. There are city-dwelling folks down here who wouldn't take an airplane to travel somewhere. But in heaven, both will be satisfied and supremely happy.

The Bible does record that the New Jerusalem is a city. But it will be a good city with no crime and no dirt, friendly people and absolutely firm rules on citizenship. You will love it. Let's stay faithful to Christ as we wait for Him to appear.

O God, You are the architect of the universe and my body and all of nature. The city You're preparing must be wonderful! Thank You for making heaven beautiful. Amen.

Day 139

All I Ever Wanted

He fulfills the desires of those who fear him;
he hears their cry and saves them.
PSALM 145:19 NIV

Have you asked God for things and He hasn't delivered? You may think that He isn't listening, doesn't care, or just can't help you. But maybe it's something else altogether. Maybe the things you're asking for aren't good for your soul, or perhaps you need to take a hard look at your motives for asking. Are they selfish? The more we get to know God, the more His desires become our desires. And when what you want lines up with what God wants, you'll hear a lot more "Yes!" from your heavenly Father.

Lord, change my heart, soften it, and remove the hard core of selfishness that often has me thinking of my own comfort and pleasure. Show me the needs of others. Show me their need for You. Amen.

Day 140

He Won't Let You Down

He didn't tiptoe around God's promise asking cautiously skeptical questions. He plunged into the promise and came up strong, ready for God, sure that God would make good on what he had said.

Romans 4:20 msg

If there is one thing you can count on for all eternity, it's that God will never let you down. Oh, you may think He has let you down or that He will in the future because something happened that you don't understand, but only God sees all and knows all. You can trust His character. You can trust that He is good. All the time. He doesn't have poor thoughts toward you—even when you mess up. Jesus already took all of that punishment. God is not mad at you. He is not disappointed in you. He looks on you with love because of Jesus. And He will never let you down.

I trust in Your goodness, God.

Day 141

Head-On

*"If you had faith no larger than a mustard seed,
you could tell this mountain to move from here to there.
And it would. Everything would be possible for you."*
MATTHEW 17:20 CEV

The Bible tells us faith is what moves mountains. Not personal ability. Not perseverance. Not even prayer. These can all play a part in facing a challenge that looks as immovable as a mountain. But it's faith in God's ability, not our own, that's the first step toward meeting a challenge head-on—then conquering it. Remind yourself of what's true about God's loving character and incomparable power. Then move toward the challenge instead of away from it. God is in control.

Lord, You are all-powerful, all-knowing, ever-loving, and always ready to work on our behalf. There is nothing that surprises You, nothing outside of Your control, nothing that You do not understand completely. We praise You for being a God in whom our faith is fully justified. There is none like You. Amen.

Day 142

Hope because of a Father

But as it is, they desire a better country, that is,
a heavenly one. Therefore God is not ashamed to be
called their God, for he has prepared for them a city.
HEBREWS 11:16 ESV

Not every person on earth has a good father. While every living human has a biological father, a male who contributed to the genetic formation of a new being, not every human has the privilege of knowing that person in a fatherly role. And many times, it would be a horrific experience if it were even possible.

But God, our heavenly Father, will replace all the old bad ideas about fathers and fill them with Himself. For all eternity, we will be with Him and enjoy the good things He has prepared for us.

Father in heaven, I look forward to sharing
Your home someday. I love You. Amen.

Day 143

Final Joy

He is so rich in kindness and grace that he purchased our freedom with the blood of his Son and forgave our sins.

EPHESIANS 1:7 NLT

The word *redemption* means to buy back. That's what God did through Jesus—He was buying us back from the dominion, the slavery, of sin. He was restoring the original relationship mankind had with Him in the perfection of Eden. He was giving us the hope of being in His eternal presence someday.

The woman who has hope for eternity knows that her redemption is only because of Christ. And she does not lose sight of that in all the other messages of the church. She holds fast to the riches of His grace and looks ahead to that perfect day.

Dear God, thank You for buying me back from destruction. Use me to tell others about this hope. In Jesus' name, amen.

Day 144
Opportunities

Anyone who meets a testing challenge head-on and manages to stick it out is mighty fortunate. For such persons loyally in love with God, the reward is life and more life.

James 1:12 MSG

People joke about how women sit around eating bonbons all day. You know firsthand nothing is farther from the truth. You face challenges each and every day. Instead of viewing challenges as negative, faith helps you see them as opportunities for growth. In the same way that strengthening your body is difficult and often uncomfortable, strengthening your faith can be the same way. But the outcome is worth the challenge. A stronger faith results in a more balanced life.

Dear Lord, thank You for helping us run the race in such a way that we will win the prize. You call us—and enable us—to run with perseverance and joy. Thank You, Jesus, for being our delight, our prize, and our sure reward. He who promises is faithful! Amen.

Day 145

A Strong Foundation Matters

"Whoever hears these words of Mine and does them, will be like a wise man who built his house on rock. The rain came down. The water came up. The wind blew and hit the house. The house did not fall because it was built on rock."
MATTHEW 7:24–25 NLV

Jesus tells this story in Matthew to teach us about life as a Christian. If we build our lives on the firm foundation of Jesus, we won't fall apart when hard things happen. We trust in God! But if we don't have a solid foundation in Jesus, not knowing or believing His truth for our lives, we can fall apart when storms and bad things happen to us. Put your trust in the solid rock of Jesus. He will never let you fall!

Jesus, I know You are my strong foundation that will be with me no matter what storms come my way.

Day 146

Intangible Crowns

"The Lord rewards people who are faithful and live right."
1 Samuel 26:23 CEV

Exactly how God rewards His children is a bit of a mystery. The Bible uses striking imagery such as golden streets and crowns being cast at Jesus' feet to honor Him. But the Bible also talks about rewards in this life. Our rewards may be delivered in tangible ways, such as through success or financial gain. But our reward may also be a more intangible treasure, such as contentment and joy. Treasures like these will never tarnish or grow old.

Lord, I ask You to fill my storehouse with the things that can never be stolen or destroyed. Love, joy, peace, patience, kindness, and self-control are rewards given by the Spirit—crowns that are a part of us and can never be taken away. Thank You for these imperishable rewards. Amen.

Day 147

Contents of a Life

No one can lay any foundation other than the one we already have—Jesus Christ. Anyone who builds on that foundation may use a variety of materials—gold, silver, jewels, wood, hay, or straw. But on the judgment day, fire will reveal what kind of work each builder has done. The fire will show if a person's work has any value.

1 CORINTHIANS 3:11–13 NLT

Going through the belongings of someone who has died is both a pitiful and an enlightening activity. The common elements of human life are there—nail clippers, safety pins, coins, writing pens, etc. But someday, at the judgment, the spiritual elements of our lives will be examined and tried by fire and only what is valuable will remain.

O judge of all the earth, show me what to value so that my life work will not be consumed as refuse. Amen.

Day 148

Trust Him

Some trust in chariots and some in horses, but we trust in the name of the Lord our God. They are brought to their knees and fall, but we rise up and stand firm.

Psalm 20:7–8 NIV

Do you hoard leftover pieces and parts because you might have a use for them one day? Our safety nets give us comfort. Whether it's money in the bank, food in the pantry, or life insurance, we have some peace of mind knowing it's there—just in case. Being prepared is never a bad idea, but scripture also warns us to be careful about placing our trust in things that will eventually fail. God is the backup plan who will never fail us. Only He can help us stand firm when life collapses. In what are you trusting?

Father, sometimes I look to my own resources and resourcefulness to save me when I should be trusting You. Help me to trust You more. Amen.

Day 149

Training in Truth

All Scripture is God-breathed and is useful for teaching, rebuking, correcting and training in righteousness.

2 TIMOTHY 3:16 NIV

The Bible tells us that our enemy, Satan, is the father of lies. He will try every trick in the book to get you to mess up. What did Jesus do when He was tempted? He told Satan the truth from God's Word. When you feel like you are being tempted to make a bad choice, ask Jesus for help. He has been there! He knows how to help you overcome. It matters to Jesus that you know there is always a way out of sin (1 Corinthians 10:13). He can help you make the right choice in the moment. When you memorize scripture, God's Spirit will help you remember those powerful words right when you need them. Start with 2 Timothy 3:16.

Jesus, when I'm tempted, remind me of Your truth.

Day 150

Ultimate Makeover

Don't become so well-adjusted to your culture that you fit into it without even thinking. Instead, fix your attention on God. You'll be changed from the inside out.

ROMANS 12:2 MSG

You're no longer the woman you once were. When you put your faith in God, you experience the ultimate makeover. You're totally forgiven. You're empowered to be able to do whatever God asks. Your old habits lose their grip over you. But continued growth and change is a joint effort between you and God. If there's any area in your life that seems resistant to change, talk to God about it right now—and every morning until change takes place.

Lord, I praise You that I am not who I once was. I was condemned; now I am redeemed. I was lost; now I am found. I was blind; now I can see. The world looks different, Lord, and sometimes it's painful. Help me to fix my eyes on You, no matter what. Amen.

Day 151

A Fragrant Life

But thank God! He has made us his captives and continues to lead us along in Christ's triumphal procession. Now he uses us to spread the knowledge of Christ everywhere, like a sweet perfume.

2 CORINTHIANS 2:14 NLT

One of the things you will notice about a woman's closet is that her clothing may bear her scent. After a loved one dies, the family may draw comfort from inhaling the fragrance left on things she wore. The scent reminds them of the loveliness of her life.

In a similar way, the lives we lead as believers leave a scent behind us. The attitudes and actions we had remain in the memories of those who knew us and remind them of us. Of course, all of us are human and therefore have moments of deep humanity. But the overall tone of our lives can bear a sweet fragrance that ever leaves a legacy of grace.

Dear Jesus, I want my life to have the fragrance of love and service like Yours. Amen.

Day 152

When Words Fail

And the Holy Spirit helps us in our weakness. For example, we don't know what God wants us to pray for. But the Holy Spirit prays for us with groanings that cannot be expressed in words.
ROMANS 8:26 NLT

This verse is a warm hug to the troubled heart. Sometimes life is confusing and hard circumstances push us around. We don't know what to do or even what to ask God for. But it's okay, because the Holy Spirit knows exactly what to say, and He passionately prays for us. He is our greatest prayer warrior.

Lord, it soothes my anxiety to know that You so completely care for me in my human weakness. Even when I'm too confused and helpless to pray, You fill the gap with prayers on my behalf. Amen.

Day 153

"Adieu!"

"Forget the former things; do not dwell on the past. See, I am doing a new thing! Now it springs up; do you not perceive it?"
Isaiah 43:18–19 NIV

Change is a combination of embracing and letting go. When you become a mom, you welcome new love and bid "adieu" to some former freedoms. When you put your faith in God, you embrace the guidance of God's Spirit and abandon your old, self-centered agenda. When times get tough, it's tempting to seek comfort by looking to the past. But life only moves in one direction—forward. Only by letting go of yesterday can you welcome today's opportunities with open arms.

Dear Father, You make all things new. You have made us new through the power of Your Spirit. Thank You for drawing us. Thank You for redeeming us. Thank You for sanctifying us. Thank You for giving us the power to lay down our sins and pick up our crosses daily. Amen.

Day 154

Perfect Peace

"I have told you these things, so that in Me you may have [perfect] peace. In the world you have tribulation and distress and suffering, but be courageous [be confident, be undaunted, be filled with joy]; I have overcome the world." [My conquest is accomplished, My victory abiding.]

John 16:33 AMP

The world God created is a beautiful place, but it's a messed up place too. We live in a fallen world, and things won't be perfect again until Jesus returns. Jesus promises us that this world will have trouble because it's not heaven. We can't expect it to be. It's time to let go of your expectations of what this world should be. Embrace the reality and goodness of God's peace and presence in the midst of a dark world.

Jesus, I want the perfect peace that only You offer. May I embrace the reality that You are here to help me through this life with Your peace.

Day 155

Desired Reward

It is impossible to please God without faith. Anyone who wants to come to him must believe that God exists and that he rewards those who sincerely seek him.

HEBREWS 11:6 NLT

Ultimately, it's not what you do, but what you believe that's rewarded by God. You can fill your life with good deeds, even to the point of sacrificing your life. But if your faith is in your own strength, abilities, or goodness—instead of in God—your full reward will be the praise of those around you. However, if you're motivated by faith, the only reward you'll desire is pleasing God. Having faith in God truly is its own reward.

Dear Lord, we need a daily reminder that we can't please You without faith. Our good deeds do nothing to earn our salvation. They are only ever the fruit of our belief. Thank You that faith is enough to save us; thank You that faith also leads to action. Amen.

Day 156

Time to Rest

It is useless for you to work so hard from early morning until late at night, anxiously working for food to eat; for God gives rest to his loved ones.

Psalm 127:2 NLT

For three years, Jesus devoted His life to spreading the good news about God's love. This was an incredibly important job, one with eternal consequences. But even Jesus took time to rest. Although He dined with friends, taught, preached, and performed miracles, many times He left spiritually hungry crowds behind to spend time alone with His heavenly Father. You have many important roles to fill in this life. Rest is one of God's gifts that can empower you to accomplish what He's given you to do.

Lord, You know me. You know that I start every day with a to-do list and how much pleasure I get in checking things off. You know how "unproductive" activities irritate me. But You give rest to Your loved ones. Thank You for this timely reminder to stop. Amen.

Day 157

A Story to Tell

Give her of the fruit of her hands, and let her own works praise her in the gates [of the city]!
PROVERBS 31:31 AMPC

All of us are good at something, and when we go to be with Jesus someday, those we leave will look through our things and remember what we did. The possessions we have will tell a story about us.

A woman who wants to leave a legacy of hope will use her talents in ways that glorify the God who gave them and that bless others around her. And someday when they stand around her casket, they'll have more to say than "Doesn't she look good!"

Dear Lord, live Your life through my abilities and let me use them to honor You. Amen.

Day 158

Power and Love

But the Lord is the true God. He is the living God and the King Who lives forever. . . . It is He Who made the earth by His power, and the world by His wisdom. By His understanding He has spread out the heavens. When He speaks, there is a storm of waters in the heavens. He makes the clouds rise from the ends of the earth. He makes lightning for the rain, and brings out the wind from His store-houses.

JEREMIAH 10:10, 12–13 NLV

The God who loves and cares about you is the same God who stretched out the heavens. It might be hard to believe that you matter so much to God, but the Bible tells us it's true. When you think about God's unlimited power and His love for you, do you trust that God can handle anything you have going on?

Father, if You can speak water into existence at the sound of Your voice, I know You can take care of anything that comes my way.

Day 159
Parts of Speech

May the words of my mouth and the meditation of my heart be pleasing to you, O LORD, my rock and my redeemer.
PSALM 19:14 NLT

There is hope for your legacy when you guard the words of your mouth and the meditations of your mind. Careless speech, sown to the wind, does not profit anyone and certainly does not stand the test of time. But words that are passed through the oversight of the Holy Spirit will have lasting effect and will grace the memory of those who knew you.

Legacy words are thoughtful and purposeful, sometimes strong, sometimes quiet, but always with the purpose of instructing others in the way of righteousness. These words will live on when we do not.

Lord in heaven, You created speech with all its expressions and modifiers and participles and prepositions and nuances. Today, let me use my language to leave a legacy. Amen.

Day 160

What Counts

And he shall be like a tree firmly planted [and tended] by the streams of water, ready to bring forth its fruit in its season; its leaf also shall not fade or wither; and everything he does shall prosper [and come to maturity]. Not so the wicked [those disobedient and living without God are not so]. But they are like the chaff [worthless, dead, without substance] which the wind drives away.

PSALM 1:3–4 AMPC

There is no significance to chaff—it is refuse, litter, worthless. Both in the wheat field and in a life, whatever is chaff does not add anything of note. Too many women are living their lives in chaffy ways and building for themselves a life of no lasting significance.

The way to have a significant legacy is to be like a tree planted in God, and then everything we do for Him will prosper.

Father in heaven, keep me today from worthless living. I want my life to count. Amen.

Day 161

His Company

"Are you tired? Worn out? Burned out on religion? Come to me. Get away with me and you'll recover your life. I'll show you how to take a real rest."

MATTHEW 11:28–29 MSG

Faith is not a to-do list of assignments from God; it's an invitation to relationship. It's about getting to know who God is and who He created you to be. It's about resting in God's love and acceptance, not working harder to prove yourself worthy of His affection. If you're suffering from spiritual burnout, take time to simply relax in God's presence, enjoying His company the way He enjoys yours.

Dear Lord, we have a hard time resting in Jesus' accomplishment on our behalf; we want to "deserve" our salvation by doing something as well. Help us to rest, rejoicing, in the finished work of Christ. We can add nothing to it except praise and thanksgiving. Amen.

Day 162

Ultimate Authority Figure

Everything you were taught can be put into a few words: Respect and obey God! This is what life is all about.
Ecclesiastes 12:13 CEV

As a little girl, chances are you were taught to respect authority. Parents, teachers, police officers, the elderly—people whose relationship, experience, or profession put them in a position of influence over your life—were deemed worthy of honor and obedience. Now, as a woman of faith, you've accepted God as the ultimate authority figure over you. Don't let that title scare you. God's love tempers the power of His position. Respecting Him is just one more way of worshipping Him.

Lord, You are the Creator of the galaxies, and Your hand keeps them spinning in perfect motion. You are the source of life and sent Your only Son to die for our sins so we could share in that life. Help us to grow in knowledge, respect, obedience, and worship. Amen.

Day 163

Testing. . .

Test yourselves and find out if you really are true to your faith. If you pass the test, you will discover that Christ is living in you.
2 CORINTHIANS 13:5 CEV

As a kid, you took plenty of tests. Your GPA was determined by how your efforts measured up to a set standard. As a woman of faith, it's time for another test: measure your character against the woman God desires you to become. This isn't a test God grades. It's simply a tool to help you know where your faith needs to grow. Best of all, this is a group project. Jesus is working both in you and through you.

Lord, You live in me! If that isn't a reason to shout, sing, and dance, then nothing is! I know I'm not who You want me to be yet; but, praise God, I'm not who I once was. Help me to keep my eyes fixed on Jesus—my model, my guide, and my friend. Amen.

Day 164

God Sings

"The L*ORD your God is with you, the Mighty Warrior who saves. He will take great delight in you; in his love he will no longer rebuke you, but will rejoice over you with singing."*

ZEPHANIAH 3:17 NIV

Getting to know God through reading His Word and prayer will change your life. He changes your thoughts to match His thoughts. As you get to know God, you will find that He's so much more than you ever thought possible. He is all-knowing, all-powerful, the Savior of the world—and yet the Bible tells us that He sings over us! God delights in You. He sees you through the eyes of Jesus. Nothing can make Him love you more or less. You cannot work for God's love. It just is.

Lord, I want to know Your words and Your truth for my life. I accept Your great love for me.

Day 165

Perfectly Content

But godliness with contentment is great gain. For we brought nothing into the world, and we can take nothing out of it. But if we have food and clothing, we will be content with that.

1 TIMOTHY 6:6–8 NIV

We often tell ourselves that life would be grander if only we had more—more things, more time, more money, more popularity. If only we were smarter, thinner, prettier, life would be a breeze. But God has a different way of doing things, of more peace and less striving. Lay aside your grasping for more and simply be happy with the things you have. Don't know where to begin? Start small and thank God for every good thing you can see from where you're sitting.

God, thank You for the blessing of the sun that came up this morning. Thank You for another day to bring glory to Your name. Amen.

Day 166

Face-to-Face

"Righteous Father, though the world does not know you, I know you, and they know that you have sent me. I have made you known to them, and will continue to make you known in order that the love you have for me may be in them and that I myself may be in them."

JOHN 17:25–26 NIV

Jesus came to show us what God is like—to introduce us face-to-face to the God who is our Father and who loves us deeply. He longs to heal our hurts and be with us. Jesus lived out God's character right in front of us. And His greatest act of kindness was the sacrifice of Jesus to pay for our sins. Now that you've met Him, are you living out His love to others?

Father, thank You for Jesus. Help me to treat everyone I encounter with Your love. Amen.

Day 167

A Lasting Imprint

He makes the barren woman to be a homemaker and a joyful mother of [spiritual] children. Praise the Lord! (Hallelujah!)

Psalm 113:9 AMPC

Leaving a legacy is important, especially as a child of God.

We will leave a legacy whether we try to or not. The log of our actions and words and decisions and interactions will be recorded in the memories of those who knew us. How wonderful if that log is defined by a heart for God and a commitment to His ways!

One of the ways a Christian woman leaves a legacy is through the spiritual children she nurtures. Even if she is not a biological mother, she may be a spiritual mother, leaving a lasting imprint on the lives of those she nurtured in the faith.

God of all grace, let Your love so fill me that I may be a spiritual mother to many who come after me. Amen.

Day 168

Courage in a Martha World

But the Lord said to her, "My dear Martha, you are worried and upset over all these details! There is only one thing worth being concerned about. Mary has discovered it, and it will not be taken away from her."

LUKE 10:41–42 NLT

You know the story. Martha was busy in the kitchen doing what women "should" do. Mary was sitting at Jesus' feet. Martha did what was expected, and Mary went against the cultural norms to be with Jesus. This made Martha mad. Jesus replied in love to Martha, but He also told her the truth. Mary made the better choice. It's hard to go against the norms and follow Jesus. Ask Jesus for courage to follow Him even when everyone else says you're making the wrong choice.

Lord, please give me the courage to be a Mary in a Martha world.

Day 169

Unblemished

Once you were alienated from God and were enemies in your minds because of your evil behavior. But now he has reconciled you by Christ's physical body through death to present you holy in his sight, without blemish and free from accusation.

COLOSSIANS 1:21–22 NIV

Actions speak louder than words. We say that we're following Jesus, but are we living our faith by choosing God's way over sin? Of course we're all human, which means we all fail sometimes or convince ourselves that what we're doing isn't really that bad. Modern culture makes light of sin and labels it with less offensive titles, like little "white lies" and the "right to choose"—but ultimately, any alternative to God leads only to death. Have you continued to indulge bad habits or lack of self-control?

Lord, forgive me for allowing my sinful impulses to control me. Give me strength and courage to choose right over wrong. Amen.

Day 170

Resting in Eternal Embrace

And I heard a voice from heaven saying, "Write this down: Blessed are those who die in the Lord from now on. Yes, says the Spirit, they are blessed indeed, for they will rest from their hard work; for their good deeds follow them!"

REVELATION 14:13 NLT

The Bible is clear that when we are absent from our earthly bodies, we are in God's eternal presence. The liturgy for a graveside ceremony may reference the fact that the body is resting until the final resurrection. And while the dust of the body lies in the ground, the spirit of the believer is resting in the eternal embrace of the one who made her and died for her. This is the truest kind of rest there can be.

Heavenly Lord, I want to rest in You for eternity and share Your heaven. Thank You for making that possible through Jesus. In His name, amen.

Day 171

Limitless

Lord, you know the hopes of the helpless.
Surely you will hear their cries and comfort them.
Psalm 10:17 NLT

There's only so much one woman can do. There are limits to your strength, your time, and your capacity to love others well. When you reach the limit of your own abilities, a feeling of helplessness can set in. But being helpless isn't synonymous with being hopeless. God is near. He hears every prayer, every longing, and every sigh. His power, love, and time are limitless. Cry out in faith when you need the comfort of your Father's love.

Lord, we praise You for being a God of love. And not only do You love us but You are so replete with love that it overflows from us to everyone around us. That's not something we can do in our own strength. But when we feel like we can't love anymore, You can. Amen.

Day 172

Alive in Creation

I will sing of the loving-kindness of the Lord forever. I will make known with my mouth how faithful You are to all people. . . . The heavens are Yours; and the earth is Yours. You have made the world and all that is in it.

Psalm 89:1, 11 NLV

One of the simplest ways to actually see God's love is to go outside and experience His creation for yourself. You can see His handiwork in the flowers and trees in spring and summer. He reveals His majesty in the bright leaves showering down in the fall and in the blankets of snow He sends in the winter. Animals and creatures great and small know their Creator. The birds God created are always singing His praises as they go about their busy tasks—and you can too. God gave you your voice to talk to Him, to tell of His great love, and to sing His praises.

Thanks for showing Your love for me through Your creation, Father. I love to sing Your praises.

Day 173

Desperate Measures

But as for me, I am poor and needy; please hurry to my aid,
O God. You are my helper and my savior; O LORD, do not delay.
PSALM 70:5 NLT

Our fears often torment our minds. What if I lose my job and can't afford to survive? What if I get sick and can't care for my children? Maybe you spend anxious hours pondering contingency plans for catastrophes that haven't happened, or perhaps you're living in the midst of tragedy and heartbreak. Desperation is never a good feeling. Job was assaulted with one agonizing loss after another, but his faith in God's love and goodness never wavered. And God is your help too.

Father, when I need You, hurry to help me. Give me courage and faith that You are mighty to save. Amen.

Day 174

Reality Check

"I am the Lord, who made all things. I alone stretched out the heavens. Who was with me when I made the earth?"

Isaiah 44:24 NLT

Raise your hand if you're an obsessed-with-every-detail perfectionist. If people are staring, I apologize. Maybe you're not a perfectionist at all, but you probably know one. Perfectionism is a mind plague that, if left unchecked, can convince us that we can handle God's job better than He can. That's when we need a reality check—He is God and we are not. Details are not bad. God blesses some people with the gift of organization, but don't get caught up in thinking that God needs us to whip all the pieces in place for His plan to succeed. Take a rest from your obsession. God's got this.

Lord God, You are the all-powerful God of the universe. Increase my trust in You. Amen.

Day 175

Vacations for Body and Mind

Jesus said, "Let's go off by ourselves to a quiet place and rest awhile." He said this because there were so many people coming and going that Jesus and his apostles didn't even have time to eat.

MARK 6:31 NLT

Vacations are the bright spots on our calendars. We look forward to them all year.

Jesus knew that His disciples needed a little while away from the work of ministry so that they could eat in peace and rest themselves, physically and spiritually. We need that too. Being a woman of hope, a woman of rest, means being realistic about appropriate self-care. A vacation should be on the list.

Lord God, You know the rest I need.
Help me to plan a restful vacation this year. Amen.

Day 176

Wonderfully Made

Your eyes saw me before I was put together. And all the days of my life were written in Your book before any of them came to be.
PSALM 139:16 NLV

Check out what the Bible says about you in Psalm 139:13–14 (NIV): "For you created my inmost being; you knit me together in my mother's womb. I praise you because I am fearfully and wonderfully made; your works are wonderful, I know that full well." Imagine Jesus putting you together before you were born. He knows everything about you, and He cares for you more than anything else in creation. The next time you're feeling down or unimportant or lonely, remember who made you and how much He loves you!

Jesus, You made me wonderfully. I accept that and rejoice in who You made me to be. You see me, Lord. And I love You.

Day 177

Changed Hearts

Such things were written in the Scriptures long ago to teach us. And the Scriptures give us hope and encouragement as we wait patiently for God's promises to be fulfilled.

Romans 15:4 NLT

Reading how women like us have faced difficult circumstances, yet found peace, power, and purpose through faith can be a source of comfort. Whether the account is about Lazarus' sisters Mary and Martha, the woman caught in adultery, or the Samaritan at the well, these women all found comfort in Christ's words. In turn, we can be comforted by their experience. Just as Christ changed their hearts and lives, His words and His love can do the same for us today.

But Lord, for us to be changed by Your Word, we have to consume it. Give us a hunger to read it; help us choose what is best over what is merely good. Your Word is life, truth, peace, and wisdom. We need all those things so much. We need You, Lord. Amen.

Day 178

Defined by Jesus

I have been crucified with Christ and I no longer live, but Christ lives in me. The life I now live in the body, I live by faith in the Son of God, who loved me and gave himself for me.

GALATIANS 2:20 NIV

What defines you? Usually when someone asks about us, we answer with what we do. "I'm a teacher." "I'm a mom." But is this the true essence of who you are? The apostle Paul wrote that "you died, and your life is now hidden with Christ in God" (Colossians 3:3 NIV). Would *Christlike* be the first adjective that people use for you? Too often we waste a lot of effort trying to "find ourselves," but there's only Jesus. How can you be defined by Jesus today?

Father, keep me from finding my sense of worth in my accomplishments. My true identity is found only in Jesus' work on the cross. Amen.

Day 179

Cadence and Gratitude

You shall come to your grave in ripe old age,
like a sheaf gathered up in its season.
Job 5:26 ESV

There is a kind of death that though sad and unwelcome as the curse always is, reminds us that God finishes what He begins. . .and that a life well lived has a fitting ending. These are the types of graves that are graced with a tombstone that captions a life that was lived long and righteously, full of adventure and promise, influencing others to do good things and ending in a dignified, quiet manner. This is the type of death we would all prefer, but which only some are granted. But they remind us that in God's hands, even the results of a curse can be redeemed and beautified.

God of the Ages, thank You for providing the cadence to the end of life as well as to the beginning. I trust You for the details of mine. Amen.

Day 180

Rested and Ready

The Lord is my light and my salvation—so why should I be afraid? The Lord is my fortress, protecting me from danger, so why should I tremble?

Psalm 27:1 NLT

The mind is a powerful entity, and it exerts tremendous sway over the whole body. If one believes she cannot do a thing, whether it be ice skating or baking a cake, her body will absorb her opinion and she probably won't.

God's Word reminds us that we have nothing to fear when He is the strength of our lives. Spiritual rest comes from putting absolute confidence in His ability to shore up our inability.

God my Father, I am always amazed at the strength I gain from being in Your presence. When I do, my mind is rested and ready to take up the next challenge. I gladly owe my rest to You. Amen.

Day 181

Life Preserver

Cling to your faith in Christ.

1 TIMOTHY 1:19 NLT

If you were shipwrecked, you'd cling to your life preserver in hope of rescue. Faith is your life preserver in this world. It keeps your head above water in life and carries you safely into God's arms after death. But it takes commitment to keep holding on tight. Emotions rise and fall. Circumstances ebb and flow. But God is committed to you. His love and faithfulness never fail. By holding tightly to your faith, you can weather any storm.

Dear Lord, thank You that at the same time I am holding on to You, You are holding on to me. Your arms are strong and tireless, and I can rest in the knowledge that You will never let me go. Help me press into You deeper and cling tighter. Amen.

Day 182

The Power of Prayer

Therefore, confess your sins to one another [your false steps, your offenses], and pray for one another, that you may be healed and restored. The heartfelt and persistent prayer of a righteous man (believer) can accomplish much [when put into action and made effective by God—it is dynamic and can have tremendous power].

JAMES 5:16 AMP

Prayer is very powerful. Not only do we get to know God better when we talk to Him, but our prayers can make things happen. God's Word tells us to pray for others so that they can be healed and restored. This means not only that physical bodies can be healed, but that broken hearts can be fixed. Bring whatever is on your heart today to Jesus for healing. What friends and family members need His loving touch? Your prayers can make all the difference!

Lord, please increase my faith in the power of prayer.

Day 183

Rest and Enjoy

There is nothing better for a man than that he should eat and drink and make himself enjoy good in his labor. Even this, I have seen, is from the hand of God.

ECCLESIASTES 2:24 AMPC

Because our lives usually run on the scale of global proportions, we forget to find enjoyment in the ordinary. But when we do, that's a kind of rest.

Through the means of technology, we are exposed to the high highs and low lows of people from all over the world. Our own little bits of happiness in our homes and gardens and favorite easy chairs can seem paltry in comparison. But the wise man was inspired to remind us that these simple pleasures are the gift of God. And when we enjoy them, we enter into a type of rest that is good and blessed.

Thank You, O God, for creating simple pleasures. I will enjoy them with a full heart. Amen.

Day 184

Joyful Hope

Why spend money on what is not bread, and your labor on what does not satisfy? Listen, listen to me, and eat what is good, and you will delight in the richest of fare.

ISAIAH 55:2 NIV

Christmas has always been my mother's favorite holiday. Her joy is infectious, and her giddiness childlike. She gives great attention to every detail in preparing for this special day: the most delicious food, ribbon-embellished packages stacked artfully beneath a glowing tree, family gatherings, and smiles. The promise of good things at Christmas brings joyful expectation. How would it affect our lives if we brought this same insatiable delight into every day as we look with joyful hope toward eternity? Today, allow your thrilling hope of heaven to propel you to drop any worthless things you've been pursuing.

Father, what dissatisfying things am I using to find happiness? Fill me with the joy of hope! Amen.

Day 185

Written on Your Heart

"This is the covenant I will make with the people of Israel after that time," declares the Lord. "I will put my law in their minds and write it on their hearts. I will be their God, and they will be my people."

Jeremiah 31:33 NIV

This new covenant begins with Jesus. Before Him, God's laws were written on stone tablets and scrolls, but through His Son's sacrifice, His ways are now etched into the hearts of all believers by the Holy Spirit. And our loving Father knows that the things that hold our attention and affections lie close to our hearts. As Matthew Henry wrote in his commentary, we should pray "that our duty may be done conscientiously and with delight." And with this promise comes relationship—He will be our all-sufficient God.

Lord, strengthen my desire and my delight in obeying You. Amen.

Day 186

When, Not If

When I am afraid, I put my trust in you. In God, whose word I praise, in God I trust; I shall not be afraid.
Psalm 56:3–4 ESV

It is interesting that the wording of this verse is "when" and not "if." It seems that the Bible acknowledges that there will be moments when the uncertainties of this earthly life will cause the emotion of fear to rise up inside us. But what we do with our fear is what matters. When we feel the rise of fear, we must meet it with an equal measure of trust. This is not a trust that nothing bad will ever happen; it's a trust that when it does, we will not be alone—a trust that says He is in charge and nothing is random.

O God, there is no one more trustworthy than You. I place my life in Your hands. Amen.

Day 187

Follow Through

By faith the walls of Jericho fell, after the army had marched around them for seven days.

HEBREWS 11:30 NIV

In the Bible, God asks people to do some pretty unlikely things. Build an ark. Defeat Jericho by walking around its walls. Battle a giant with a slingshot. But when people are committed to doing what God asks, amazing things happen. What's God asking you to do? Love someone who seems unlovable? Break a bad habit? Forgive? Commit yourself to follow through and do what God asks. Through faith, you'll witness firsthand how the unbelievable can happen.

Dear Father, You never ask us to do anything that You do not also give us the means to accomplish. All is possible through Your strength. Help us see not impossibilities but miraculous possibilities! Walls, giants, and sins will fall at the sound of Your voice. Amen.

Day 188

Your Tears Matter

You have taken account of my wanderings;
put my tears in Your bottle. Are they not recorded in
Your book? Then my enemies will turn back in the
day when I call; this I know, that God is for me.
PSALM 56:8–9 AMP

God cares about the things that you care about. The Bible says He even counts your tears and writes them down. In the Old Testament, Jesus was referred to as the "man of sorrows" because He was rejected by people (even some of His own friends) and was very familiar with pain and sadness. Whatever you're going through, Jesus understands because He's been there. Have you ever felt left out or not good enough for other people? Talk to God about it. Your tears matter to Him.

Lord, thank You for Your promises. I'm so glad that You are with me and that You care about my heart. Thank You for Your comfort and healing.

Day 189

In Style

As God's chosen people, holy and dearly loved, clothe yourselves with compassion, kindness, humility, gentleness and patience.

COLOSSIANS 3:12 NIV

Before you the leave the house, chances are you make sure you're appropriately dressed. You don't head out to a business meeting in your pj's, to the grocery store in your swimsuit, or off for a jog in heels. Faith offers you a different kind of wardrobe, one that's appropriate for every occasion. By clothing yourself in compassion, you reflect God's very own style—a style that always looks good on you and compliments everyone you meet.

Lord, those things—compassion, kindness, humility, gentleness, and patience—do not come naturally to me. Forgive me for the judgment, unkindness, impatience, and pride that I so often exhibit instead. I ask Your Spirit to clothe me in godly garments as I venture out into the world. Amen.

Day 190

Enduring Love

Give thanks to the God of heaven,
for his steadfast love endures forever.
PSALM 136:26 ESV

The steadfast love of God endures forever—marinate your mind in this truth for a moment. God's love for you is unfaltering, dear one. He isn't a fair-weather friend. No, His love isn't dependent on our actions. Thank goodness, because my measure would have run out long ago! His love stands forever. It's been tried and can endure anything. No matter what you've done or what has been done to you, whether you've suffered or caused suffering for others, God loves you. "God shows his love for us in that while we were still sinners, Christ died for us" (Romans 5:8 ESV). Allow God's love to permeate your mind and direct your actions.

Father, Your Word says that if I know You I will love others. Teach me to love as unconditionally as You do. Amen.

Day 191

Strength in Waiting

Wait for the Lord; be strong, and let your heart take courage; wait for the Lord!
Psalm 27:14 ESV

Waiting is tough. God promised the Israelites a new homeland when they fled Egypt, but not right away. "So the land will not become a waste, and the animals of the field become too many for you. I will drive them out a few at a time, until you become many and take the land for your own" (Exodus 23:29–30 NLV). For our own good, God doesn't give us what we're not ready to handle. We must first learn obedience so we can avoid unwanted side effects that come from impatience and poor prep work—like being overrun by wild animals!

Father, teach me to wait and grow in faith while trusting You to bring Your plans to fruition. Amen.

Day 192

Haters in Heart

Everyone who hates his brother is a murderer, and you know that no murderer has eternal life abiding in him.

1 John 3:15 ESV

The word *hate* is used a lot and often in ways that do not truly reflect the strong meaning of the word. We can hate anything from soggy bread to traffic jams. Often when we use the word, we really mean that we are irritated by something.

But the animosity and malice of real hatred for another person is strongly condemned by the Bible. There is no way that any of us can harbor hatred for someone and still follow Christ. Hating makes a murderer in spirit.

We can be women of hope by surrendering our strong emotions to God and allowing His transforming power to be revealed in us.

God, You are perfectly loving, even toward those who curse You. Give me power not to hate anyone. In Jesus' name, amen.

Day 193

In All Things

"You're blessed when you get your inside world—your mind and heart—put right. Then you can see God in the outside world."
MATTHEW 5:8 MSG

The Bible talks a lot about being "blessed" and having joy. When Jesus talks about having joy, He's talking about a deep understanding that Jesus is with us and making everything right—no matter what. That means that even if circumstances seem dire, you can still have joy. Why? Because of this promise from God right here: "And we know that in all things God works for the good of those who love him, who have been called according to his purpose" (Romans 8:28 NIV). Commit this verse to memory. It will come in handy every day of your life. God really is working all things out for your good, even when things seem all wrong.

Jesus, Help me to trust that You're working everything out for my good.

Day 194

God-Confidence

Forget about self-confidence;
it's useless. Cultivate God-confidence.
1 CORINTHIANS 10:12 MSG

You're a beautiful, gifted woman. God created you that way. You have countless reasons to be confident in what you do, who you are, and where you're headed—but those reasons don't rest on your talents, intelligence, accomplishments, net worth, or good looks. They rest solely on God and His faithfulness. Living a life of faith means trading self-confidence for God-confidence. It means holding your head high because you know you're loved and that God's Spirit is working through you.

Father God, when I despair of my sin, I remember that Jesus has paid for it all. When I fear death, I remember that Jesus has overcome it. When I sigh at my limitations, I remember that You created me. And when I flirt with pride, I remember that I am Your creation. Amen.

Day 195

Finding Truth

"I the Lord speak the truth; I declare what is right."

Isaiah 45:19 ESV

God created every square inch of this universe, and He also equipped us with the tools we need to identify what is truth. We can experience truth through our senses, we can use the minds He gave us to reason, and we can learn from others who know truth. But some truths can be revealed to us only by God. And He never lies—it's not part of His character (1 Samuel 15:29). Examine the messages behind the words and images you encounter today. Ask yourself if the ideas being communicated are true, half true, or total falsehoods.

Father, give me the wisdom through Your Word to identify truth in this world so I'm not led astray by lies. Thank You for always telling me the truth. In the midst of confusion or hurt, I can trust You to tell me the truth. Amen.

Day 196

More of Him

"What good will it be for someone to gain the whole world, yet forfeit their soul? Or what can anyone give in exchange for their soul?"
MATTHEW 16:26 NIV

It seems there's never enough money to satisfy our desires. If we get a raise or an unexpected bonus, we already have plans for the money and what we would do with even more—luxurious vacations, bigger homes, expensive shoes. Our desires can really run wild. But Jesus says that no matter how much stuff we can afford, or wish we could, He is the most important. Today, when you talk to God in prayer, instead of asking Him for things you wish you had, ask for more of Jesus—more talks with Him, more prayer, more time in scripture.

Father, I need more of You in my life. Give me more love, patience, understanding, and forgiveness for others. Amen.

Day 197

Awed

The Fear-of-God builds up confidence,
and makes a world safe for your children.
Proverbs 14:26 MSG

When the Bible talks about the "fear of God," it's more about awe than alarm. Through faith, we catch a glimpse of how powerful God really is and how small we are in comparison. Yet the depth of God's love for us rivals the enormity of His might. Regardless of the troubles that may surround you or what you see on the evening news, you can be confident that God remains in charge, in control, and deeply in love.

Dear Lord, we stand amazed at Your provision, Your promises, Your protection, and Your peace. There is nothing in this life we need to fear but You. Help us to stand with confidence, awe, reverence, and holy fear on the Rock of our salvation. In praise and thanksgiving, amen.

Day 198

When You're Not Feelin' It

Meanwhile, the moment we get tired in the waiting, God's Spirit is right alongside helping us along. If we don't know how or what to pray, it doesn't matter. He does our praying in and for us, making prayer out of our wordless sighs, our aching groans. He knows us far better than we know ourselves. . .and keeps us present before God.

Romans 8:26–27 msg

Some days you don't feel like praying. You're not alone. Jesus is very aware of the human condition because He became one of us. God knows how you feel and why. That's why He sent His Spirit to live inside of us—to encourage us always. The Spirit of God will pray in us and for us when we don't know what to pray for. . .or when we just don't feel like it. If you are feeling this way today, just sit quietly somewhere and breathe. Ask the Holy Spirit to pray for you.

Father, I thank You for sending Your Spirit to pray for me. You knew how much I would need that.

Day 199

Meet Anger at the Door

And "don't sin by letting anger control you." Don't let the sun go down while you are still angry.
Ephesians 4:26 NLT

Anger is a normal human emotion in response to an injustice, real or perceived. There are appropriate times to be angry—when an innocent person is mistreated or when someone in authority is abusive or when God's laws are being mocked by evildoers.

But there are also inappropriate angry responses that are predicated on our own selfish wishes or perceived rights. When we are angry because someone didn't fulfill our expectations or made us look bad or caused us inconvenience, we must be careful to sort out our motivation for response and choose to follow what the Spirit is saying.

Feelings of anger must be met at the door by truth and temperance.

Lord Jesus, You had so many reasons to be angry while You were on earth, but You never expressed it in unholy ways. Help me to follow Your example. Amen.

Day 200

He Is My Strength

But he said to me, "My grace is sufficient for you, for my power is made perfect in weakness." Therefore I will boast all the more gladly about my weaknesses, so that Christ's power may rest on me.

2 CORINTHIANS 12:9 NIV

Everyone has days when their strength doesn't seem sufficient to stretch to evening—when pulling the covers back over your head is an enticing thought. Impatience and snappish words come to the fore when work is overwhelming, the kids misbehave, the laundry forms mountains, and everyone's hungry. I know that I can't deal with all this alone. But through Christ I can! He is mighty when I feel like I might break. He has chosen you to be His instrument. Trust Him, and He'll be strong for you.

Lord, thank You for being strong for me. I don't have to do it alone or hold everything together. That's Your job. Amen.

Day 201

Heart and Mind

Men cannot say they do not know about God.
From the beginning of the world, men could see what
God is like through the things He has made. This shows
His power that lasts forever. It shows that He is God.

Romans 1:20 NLV

Today, many argue that faith in our Creator God is in conflict with the natural world around us. But astronomer, physicist, and engineer Galileo Galilei believed God gave us our minds to explore the world. He said, "The Bible shows the way to go to heaven, not the way the heavens go." We're free to pursue God's truth with both our heart and mind. But engage those who don't share your faith with humility. After all, the Bible is not a technical manual but instead a story of God's interaction with humans that points us to Christ. Love above all things.

Creator God, give me humility and understanding so that others may be drawn to Jesus. Amen.

Day 202

Path to Contentment

"You're blessed when you're content with just who you are—no more, no less. That's the moment you find yourselves proud owners of everything that can't be bought."

MATTHEW 5:5 MSG

Being content with what you have is one thing. Being content with who you are is quite another. This kind of contentment isn't complacency. It doesn't negate the importance of striving for excellence or encouraging growth and change. It means being at peace with the way God designed you and the life He's given you. This kind of contentment is only available in daily doses. Through faith, seek God and His path to contentment each and every morning.

Lord, thank You that contentment isn't having what we want but wanting what we have. And when we accept Jesus Christ as our Savior, Your Word promises that You give us everything we need for life and godliness. Everything. Everything! Remind us daily that what we need is already ours. Amen.

Day 203

New Every Morning

Because of the LORD*'s great love we are not consumed, for his compassions never fail. They are new every morning; great is your faithfulness.*

LAMENTATIONS 3:22–23 NIV

Popular *Anne of Green Gables* character Anne Shirley said, "Tomorrow is always fresh with no mistakes in it." What a great thought to remember! God's love never ends. His mercy is new every morning. Mercy is the true fact that God doesn't punish us as our sins deserve. He does this because of what Jesus did for us on the cross. So if you feel like you've failed a lot today, God has forgiven you. And you can go to sleep in peace tonight knowing that our great God has made a way for you through Jesus. God is always ready to give you a fresh start each morning.

Father, thank You for Your mercy and love that never end. I'm ready for a fresh start.

Day 204
Following the Pattern

O Lord, my heart is not lifted up; my eyes are not raised too high; I do not occupy myself with things too great and too marvelous for me.

Psalm 131:1 ESV

Arrogance usually feels repulsive to those looking on. When someone appears to think too highly of themselves and to elevate their accomplishments and opinions over others, it does not draw friends. There are times when we misjudge someone who is quiet or shy and believe she is being aloof when she is not. It is important to give everyone the benefit of the doubt.

Humility, a teachable spirit, and a ready smile will go a long way in helping us be approachable to others. When we are tempted to foster the emotion of arrogance, we must remind ourselves that as Christ followers, He is our pattern in all things.

Holy God, nothing I can do or think or say can come close to Your glory; let me stay humble as Your servant. Amen.

Day 205

Never Abandoned

"When you pass through the waters, I will be with you; and when you pass through the rivers, they will not sweep over you. When you walk through the fire, you will not be burned; the flames will not set you ablaze. For I am the LORD *your God, the Holy One of Israel, your Savior."*

ISAIAH 43:2–3 NIV

It's tempting to doubt God's love for us when we're suffering. The enemy whispers that if God really cared about us, He'd wipe away every trouble. But that isn't what scripture says. Jesus said that in this world we would definitely have trouble but that we need not worry, because He has overcome the world (John 16:33). Read slowly through today's scripture from Isaiah and sit with the knowledge that when you experience hard times, He is with you.

Father, keep my thoughts focused on the truth of Your presence with me even through the fire. Amen.

Day 206

Nothing to Fear

The blood of Jesus gives us courage to enter the most holy place by a new way that leads to life! And this way takes us through the curtain that is Christ himself.

HEBREWS 10:19–20 CEV

Imagine standing before a holy, almighty, and perfect God and being judged for how you've lived your life. Every mistake, poor choice, and moment of rebellion would be exposed. Sounds downright terrifying, doesn't it? But through our faith in Jesus, we have nothing to fear. We stand faultless and forgiven. Through Christ, we can gather the courage to look at ourselves as we really are, faults and all, without shame. Being wholly loved gives us the courage to fully live.

Lord, this is amazing grace, and it is offered to us by no other system, god, or religion. Only through Jesus Christ, whose flesh was torn for our salvation, can we be rightly seen, fully known, totally loved, and completely forgiven. We are redeemed! Praise the Lord! Amen.

Day 207

Whatever Needs Done

When I asked for your help, you answered my prayer and gave me courage.
PSALM 138:3 CEV

Why do you need courage today? To apologize? To forgive? To break an old habit? To discipline a child? To love in the face of rejection? Courage isn't just for times when you're facing grievous danger. Anytime you face difficult or unpredictable situations, it takes courage to move forward. When you're tempted to turn away from your problems, let faith help you turn toward God. With Him, you'll find the courage you need to do whatever needs to be done.

God, sometimes the things You ask me to do seem too hard. Forgive me for doubting You. I need to trust that what You call me to do, You will also equip me to accomplish. I can do all things through You. Give me the courage to step out in faith, knowing Your hands are holding me up. Amen.

Day 208

Right Here, Right Now

Better is one day in your courts than a thousand elsewhere.
PSALM 84:10 NIV

It's fun daydreaming about places you'd like to visit, goals you'd like to accomplish, or the woman you hope to mature into—someday. But God's only given you one life. Chances are, you'll have more dreams than you'll have days. Instead of living for "someday," God challenges you to put your heart into today. Whether you're sunning on vacation or scrubbing the kitchen floor, the God of the universe is right here with you. That's something worth celebrating!

Lord, thank You for the dreams and goals You have given me and how they motivate me to persevere. Thank You also for this present moment and how I can become more like You right now. Help me to live well in the tension between "already" and "not yet." Amen.

Day 209

He Won't Leave You

"Blessed be God, who has given peace to his people Israel just as he said he'd do. Not one of all those good and wonderful words that he spoke through Moses has misfired. May God, our very own God, continue to be with us just as he was with our ancestors—may he never give up and walk out on us. May he keep us centered and devoted to him, following the life path he has cleared, watching the signposts, walking at the pace and rhythms he laid down for our ancestors."

1 Kings 8:57–58 MSG

God has promised never to leave you. And only He is capable of keeping that promise to you all the days of your life. Reaffirm your trust in Him today. He is worthy of it.

Lord God, I trust Your holy and powerful words to me. You are with me. I give You my life.

Day 210

In His Image

So God created man in his own image, in the image of God he created him; male and female he created them.

Genesis 1:27 ESV

God created you in His image. And while this doesn't mean that we don't sin or that we're exactly like God, it does mean that we can see a reflection of Him in ourselves. You can see aspects of God in the way you're put together. You can catch glimpses of Him in your creativity, your appreciation for beauty, your compassion, or love of justice. So don't downplay your worth or disregard the talents God has given you. Instead, ask Him how you can use those things to bring glory to His name. Do others see Jesus superimposed over your life?

Father, help me to be a reflection of You to others. Make my life a message and a masterpiece of who You are. Amen.

Day 211

Chosen for Good Works

"Let your light shine before others, that they may see your good deeds and glorify your Father in heaven."
MATTHEW 5:16 NIV

A Catholic priest named Father Damien traveled from Belgium to Hawaii in 1873 to live at the Molokai leper colony. He was moved by compassion to help the suffering when no one else would. He worked to build houses and a church. He nursed those who were very sick and taught the people about the Bible. Eventually Father Damien also contracted leprosy and died after sixteen years on Molokai. By the time of his death, other missionaries had come to help. Father Damien glorified God by giving His life in service to others. Are you known for your good works? What can you do for others that will lead them to glorify God?

Father, let my good works be a light to others in dark places. Show me who needs my help today. Amen.

Day 212

Victory in the Mind

Wrath is cruel and anger is an overwhelming flood,
but who is able to stand before jealousy?
PROVERBS 27:4 AMPC

Feelings of jealousy or envy can come upon us like a tidal wave. In response to events taking place or the words of someone else, suddenly we feel the wave of negative and even sinful emotion rushing toward us. In that moment, we must make a choice to honor Christ both in our outward response and in the attitude we allow to remain. No one can force us to harbor feelings of jealousy or to act in un-Christlike ways.

Satan's favorite battleground on which to engage us is the mind. We need the power of the Holy Spirit and the sword of the Word in order to defeat Him.

I surrender, O Lord, my emotions to You before the moment even comes. Help me to maintain that surrender in the crisis. Amen.

Day 213

Into His Arms

"Love the Lord your God, walk in all his ways,
obey his commands, hold firmly to him, and serve
him with all your heart and all your soul."

JOSHUA 22:5 NLT

Every walk you take is a series of steps that moves you forward. Each day you live is like a single step, moving you closer to—or farther away from—God. That's why it's good to get your bearings each morning. Through reading the Bible and spending time with God in prayer, you'll know which direction to take as you continue your walk of faith. Day by day, God will guide you straight into His arms.

Dear Father, thank You for waking me early this morning to read Your Word. Thank You for the promise of a beautiful day and the sun streaming in through the windows. Thank You for these quiet minutes to draw near to You and reorient my feet. Amen.

Day 214

Eternal Perspectives

I will bless the L*ORD who guides me; even at night my heart instructs me. I know the* L*ORD is always with me. I will not be shaken, for he is right beside me. No wonder my heart is glad, and I rejoice. My body rests in safety.*

PSALM 16:7–9 NLT

With an eternal perspective, you can see problems and heartache in their proper light. Weeping may last for a little while, but joy *will* come (Psalm 30:5). Therefore, you don't have to be shaken whenever trials come. Jesus is with you always. Bring any sadness or heartache to Him. Picture yourself carrying it all to Him. He wants to help carry your load. Ask Him to help you see things through His eyes.

Jesus, I bring all of my thoughts and feelings into Your presence. Please give me Your perspective. Thank You for Your constant presence in my life. I rest my heart in You.

Day 215

Be Kind

The fruit of the Spirit is. . .kindness.
GALATIANS 5:22 NIV

Kindness often gets a bad rap. We think those who turn the other cheek are weak. But scripture tells us that God is kind—and He most certainly is not weak. Sometimes we can be a little too much like the Israelites, who had short memories for "[God's] many kindnesses" (Psalm 106:7 NIV). But God is kind, and as His children we should be too. Colossians tells us to "clothe yourselves with. . .kindness" (Colossians 3:12 NIV). Next time you encounter a rude coworker or your children trample your last nerve, remember to be kind.

Father, sometimes I struggle to be kind. I get impatient and tired and don't feel like being kind. But You have shown me kindness upon kindness that I don't deserve. Help me to go and do likewise. Amen.

Day 216

Slippery Slope of Sin

But each person is tempted when they are dragged away by their own evil desire and enticed. Then, after desire has conceived, it gives birth to sin; and sin, when it is full-grown, gives birth to death.

JAMES 1:14–16 NIV

Sin usually starts with a small concession. So scripture wisely tells us to take captive every thought and make it obedient to Christ. Joseph's brothers didn't decide to kill him out of the blue. When they indulged the sins of anger and jealousy, their hatred bloomed into a murder plot. Grievous sin always begins with one little thing: an unforgiving thought, a little white lie. . . . Have you ever let angry words fly and later regretted it? Do you have a "small" sin that you need to repent of before it grows unchecked into a bigger problem?

Heavenly Father, search my heart and show me anything in my heart and actions that goes against Your ways. Amen.

Day 217

Conversations with God

Never stop praying.

1 THESSALONIANS 5:17 NLT

Imagine the worries that would fall away if you were to live your whole life in conversation with God. The more time you spend talking to God about His desires for your life and telling Him all the amazing things you've noticed about Him, the more you will also begin to notice all the ways He answers you, gives you direction in difficult situations, or resolves a problem you had no idea how to solve. And when you're upset, there's no one better to hear your complaints. Because not only will He understand, He'll also gently confront you with truth when you need redirected. How can you live in prayer today?

Father, I want to wake up praising You for the day You've given me and fall asleep telling You about my day. And I want to talk to You every moment in between. In Jesus' name, amen.

Day 218

Rhythm of Grace

"Come to me, all you who are weary and burdened, and I will give you rest."
MATTHEW 11:28 NIV

Sometimes life seems like a race that you can never win—and you get tired. Sometimes bone-weary. Take a look at the rest of what Jesus says here in Matthew: "I'll show you how to take a real rest. Walk with me and work with me—watch how I do it. Learn the unforced rhythms of grace. I won't lay anything heavy or ill-fitting on you. Keep company with me and you'll learn to live freely and lightly" (vv. 29–30 MSG). Your busyness matters to Jesus. He wants you to come to Him and rest in Him daily, finding a new, less hurried rhythm of grace.

Jesus, please help me to find true rest and peace in You. Help me to slow down and relax.

Day 219

Root of Desire

"Wherever your treasure is, there the desires of your heart will also be."
MATTHEW 6:21 NLT

What does your heart long for? If you look at the root of every deep desire, you'll find something only God can fill. Love, security, comfort, significance, joy. . .trying to satisfy these desires apart from God can only yield limited success. God is the only one whose love for you will never waver. You're His treasure, and His desire is to spend eternity with you. As your faith grows, so will your desire to treasure Him in return.

Lord, sometimes it takes a work of Your Spirit for us to see the true roots of our desires. We long for wisdom to desire rightly, and we long for the bravery to look directly at our desires and say, "Not my will, but Yours." Help us to treasure You above all else, Father. Amen.

Day 220

Unstoppable

If God is for us, who can be against us?
Romans 8:31 ESV

It's been said that one sure way to get a chuckle from our heavenly Father is to tell Him our plans—because too often we cook them up without consulting Him. So it's no surprise that we sometimes fail in spectacular fashion. We fall. We lose. We crash and burn everything we've built and, in the process, maybe even those we love. But beloved, don't kick the ashes in defeat. Sometimes the aftermath of defeat teaches us to search out God's best for us. This verse doesn't mean we'll never fail or struggle. And it certainly doesn't mean we'll accomplish every half-baked idea that turns our head. Remember that when You're following God, nothing can stand in the way of His plans.

Father, show me the plans You have for me, plans of hope and a future. Amen.

Day 221

My Weakness, His Power

"Please, Lord, how can I save Israel? Behold, my clan is the weakest in Manasseh, and I am the least in my father's house."
JUDGES 6:15 ESV

David didn't walk out to meet Goliath because he was a mighty warrior, and Gideon didn't defeat the Midianites because he was a shrewd general. They won great victories because they trusted God when He said He was with them. Neither do you need to have significant resources or impressive skills to be used for God's purpose. God delights in working miracles through our flawed efforts to serve Him. Take a moment today and consider the interests or skills in your life that you deem small. Ask God how He could use them significantly in His kingdom.

God, I often feel small and unimportant like Gideon, but I want to trust that You can use whatever I have to do big things. Amen.

Day 222

The Perfect Harvest

The Lord longs to be gracious to you; therefore he will rise up to show you compassion. For the Lord is a God of justice. Blessed are all who wait for him!

Isaiah 30:18 NIV

God is the master of perfect timing because He can see straight across the grand scheme of history. He can tell if what you're waiting for today would be even better if it was received tomorrow—or years down the road. As you grow in your faith, you'll grow to trust God's timing more and more. Expect Him to surprise you with the perfect harvest always delivered at exactly the right time.

Lord, You see the end from the beginning. From the vantage point of heaven, our stories are already told, finished in surprising and glorious ways. Help us trust that what Your hands have written will be just what we need and desire most. In love and faith, amen.

Day 223

Significance and Stars

He determines and counts the number of the stars; He calls them all by their names.

Psalm 147:4 AMPC

The feeling of insignificance plagues the human family. We are tempted to think we are only a number, a face, another link in the infinite chain of history.

There is a company who advertises the fact that they will name a star after your friend or relative and send them a certificate for a special occasion. While we understand why someone would think that's a good idea, it is a little humorous when one considers that they have already been named by God.

And the God who names planets and heavenly bodies comprised of burning gases knows your name too. You are significant and known. That should give you hope.

Dear God, You count the stars and know where they go; You see me right now too. Thank You. Amen.

Day 224

Free Will

I pray that your love will keep on growing and you will fully know and understand how to make the right choices.

PHILIPPIANS 1:9–10 CEV

Free will is a wonderful gift. It allows you to have a say in the storyline of your life. But there are consequences tied to every decision you make, big or small. That's why making wise decisions is so important. The more you allow your faith to influence the decisions you make, the closer you'll be to living the life God desires for you. Invite God into your decision process. Let your "yes" or "no" be preceded by "amen."

Lord, thank You for this reminder that we know very little of the story You are telling with our lives. We see dimly and incompletely, at best. But we praise You for inviting us to talk to You in prayer. Remind us daily to cling to this heavenly lifeline. Amen.

Day 225

The Power Inside You

My children, you are a part of God's family. You have stood against these false preachers and had power over them. You had power over them because the One Who lives in you is stronger than the one who is in the world.

1 JOHN 4:4 NLV

The King James Version says it this way: "Greater is he that is in you, than he that is in the world." This is a powerful verse that is great to remember and say out loud whenever you're feeling afraid. Take a minute right now and write it down on a sticky note. Ask the Holy Spirit to help you memorize it. With God's power alive and at work in you, you have nothing to be afraid of. Give thanks to God that He is with you always.

Thank You for being with me all the time, Jesus. You've given me everything I need to live for You.

Day 226

Don't Turn Away

"I myself said, 'How gladly would I treat you like my children and give you a pleasant land, the most beautiful inheritance of any nation.' I thought you would call me 'Father' and not turn away from following me.'"

JEREMIAH 3:19 NIV

Toddlers have little affection for hearing the word *no*. And they often let their wishes be known in spectacular tantrum fashion. As we grow in maturity, we learn to deal with disappointment more gracefully—or so we hope. But we still don't enjoy having our wishes denied, even by our heavenly Father. Do you balk and pout when God doesn't give you the answer you want? Imagine your human understanding compared to the incalculable wisdom and love of your heavenly Father. Remembering that He sees the eternal ramifications can sweeten the bitter pill of "no."

Father, help me to follow You no matter what—to trust Your sweeping perspective. Amen.

Day 227

Trust the Truth

Jesus answered, "I am the way and the truth and the life. No one comes to the Father except through me."
JOHN 14:6 NIV

Believing that all good people go to heaven sounds nice. But it doesn't make sense. How do you measure goodness? Where's the cutoff between being "in" and being "out"? Spiritual truths cannot be relative or change according to how we feel. They must be timeless, steadfast—like Jesus. Jesus said that putting our faith in Him is the only way we can be reconciled with God and receive eternal life. Trust the truth. Trust Jesus.

Lord, it seems too simple. We want to do something to earn our salvation. But praise God, Jesus did it all on the cross, and we don't need to—and actually can't—add anything to that. Help us rest and rejoice in the finished work of Christ. Amen.

Day 228

Wholly True

Lead blameless lives and do what is right,
speaking the truth from sincere hearts.
PSALM 15:2 NLT

The truth can't be twisted or stretched. It can't masquerade as a "half truth" or a "little white lie." If what you say isn't wholly true, it isn't the truth. Period. Speaking the truth doesn't mean saying aloud every thought that enters your head. It means passing out words like gifts. Choose each one carefully. Then wrap it in love and respect. Be as honest and truthful with others as God has been with you.

Dear Father, a lie contaminates everything it touches. Forgive me for the times I have "shaded" the truth or spoken outright falsehoods. I long to speak the truth from a sincere heart, as Your Word commands. Only Your Spirit living in me can enable me to do that. Amen.

Day 229

Motivation

You are no longer ruled by your desires,
but by God's Spirit, who lives in you.
Romans 8:9 CEV

In preparing to play a role, an actress asks herself, "What's my character's motivation?" That's because what motivates us moves us. If a character's desire is to be admired, rich, beautiful, or loved, that will influence her decisions and actions. As you allow God to work in and through you, your desires begin to fall in line with His. There's no longer any need to act. You're free to be exactly who God created you to be.

Dear Father, we know nothing of the humility of infinite perfection rubbing shoulders with sinful humanity, but we praise You for being willing to live among us and in us. Give us the desire to know You better and be more fully conformed to Your image. Amen.

Day 230

A Living Hope

When we have learned not to give up, it shows we have stood the test. When we have stood the test, it gives us hope. Hope never makes us ashamed because the love of God has come into our hearts through the Holy Spirit Who was given to us.

ROMANS 5:4–5 NLV

Jesus is our living hope, and because of Him, we can have a real-life relationship with God. Our hope of heaven never goes away, but we can also have great hope and peace right now. We don't have to wait for heaven to know Him and experience His love, joy, power, and peace. He wants to give that to us now—today! God always keeps His promises, and He will be with us always. Remember, Romans 8:28 tells us that God is always working everything out for our good, even the hard things.

God, thank You for keeping Your promises and being faithful to me always.

Day 231

The Little and Big Things

Trust in the Lord with all your heart;
do not depend on your own understanding.
PROVERBS 3:5 NLT

If you lean against a wall, you have faith in its integrity. You trust it won't crumble and leave you in a heap on the floor. If you trust God, you'll lean on Him. This is more than saying, "I believe." This is living what you believe. You may not always understand the "whys" behind God's ways, but the more you risk trusting Him with the little things, the more confident you'll be trusting Him with the big ones.

Dear Lord, the longer I know You, the more I trust that what You say will come to pass. Thank You for increasing my faith through the blessings and trials You have allowed in my life. You are my strong tower, my Rock, my steady anchor. You will hold me fast. Amen.

Day 232

Joyful Service

"Whoever wants to become great among you must be your servant."
MATTHEW 20:26 NIV

Let's face it. We all want the cushy job with all the perks: the vacation home, the boat, the luxury of relaxation. It all sounds so good, and it's oh-so-easy to think only of our own fun and comfort. But Jesus doesn't measure life's success with our yardstick. Instead, He lived a life not of indulgence but of service. "Whoever wants to be first must be slave of all. For even the Son of Man did not come to be served, but to serve" (Mark 10:44–45 NIV). Do you know anyone who could use a rescue—a kind word or a little help? How can you serve them humbly in love today?

Father, show me the needs of a hurting world around me. I don't want to ignore the pain of others while I enjoy the comforts of life. Amen.

Day 233

Clean Hearts

"You are like whitewashed tombs, which look beautiful on the outside but on the inside are full of the bones of the dead and everything unclean."
MATTHEW 23:27 NIV

Jesus had harsh words for hypocrites who put all their effort into looking good but ignored the decay inside. Scripture says, "Come close to God and He will come close to you. Wash your hands, you sinners. Clean up your hearts, you who want to follow the sinful ways of the world and God at the same time" (James 4:8 NLV). We simply can't have it both ways. We can't live as the world does and follow Jesus' example at the same time. In which parts of your life might you be trying to live as the world instead of following Jesus?

Lord, keep me from spending all my time trying to look perfect for other people while allowing jealousy, pride, and selfishness to fester in my heart. Amen.

Day 234

What Lies Ahead

The word of the LORD holds true,
and we can trust everything he does.
PSALM 33:4 NLT

You confide in a friend because she's proven herself faithful over time. She won't lie. What she says she'll do, she does. You trust in her love because you believe she has your best interests at heart. God is this kind of friend. It takes time to build your own track record of trust with Him. As you do, consider His faithfulness to those in the Bible. God's past faithfulness can help you trust Him for whatever lies ahead.

Lord, it's probably a good thing that we can't see the future. Instead, like children clinging to the protective hands of a father, we hold fast to the one who holds the future. You will never fail us. What we do know is that You are faithful and will prevail. Amen.

Day 235

Faith on the Move

All the believers devoted themselves to the apostles' teaching, and to fellowship, and to sharing in meals. . . , and to prayer.

Acts 2:42 NLT

The time we set aside to read the Bible and pray each day is often called "daily devotions." Have you ever considered why? Think about what it means to be devoted to your husband, your kids, or your job. Devotion is the commitment of yourself to something or someone you love. The same is true with spiritual devotion. Your spiritual faith is a commitment to love God. And since the word *love* is both a noun and a verb—an action word—your devotion to God is faith on the move. Where will faith move you today?

Dear Lord, our faith does not only consist of us sitting in a chair and reading scripture. It's not just folding our hands and praying. That is where our faith begins, but that is not where it ends. Help us to take what we learn in prayer and turn it into action. Amen.

Day 236

Even When You Can't See

But the basic reality of God is plain enough. Open your eyes and there it is! By taking a long and thoughtful look at what God has created, people have always been able to see what their eyes as such can't see: eternal power, for instance, and the mystery of his divine being. So nobody has a good excuse.

ROMANS 1:20 MSG

Sometimes it can be hard to believe in a God we can't see. But the Bible tells us that if we take a look at creation all around us and see the amazing things He has made (including you and all the other humans around you), we are without excuse when it comes to knowing that God is real.

Bring to mind friends or family members who don't believe in God. Pray that God would open up their eyes to see Him in creation.

Open the eyes of ______, Lord.
Give me courage to share my faith with them.

Day 237

Closer Than You Think

The eyes of the Lord are on those who do what is right and good. His ears are open to their cry. . . . The Lord is near to those who have a broken heart. And He saves those who are broken in spirit.

PSALM 34:15, 18 NLV

Jesus is closer than you think. When your heart is broken, He is with you. When your spirit feels crushed, God is close. God's Word says that He hears your prayers and that His eyes are on you. He sees you. You are important to God, and He loves you more than you could ever imagine. Sometimes God will send someone to give you an extra-special dose of love at just the right time. Sometimes He will supernaturally warm your heart with love as you talk to Him. Be on the lookout for His love.

Jesus, open my eyes to see You more and know that You are near.

Day 238

Devoted to Others

Women who claim to be devoted to God should make themselves attractive by the good things they do.

1 TIMOTHY 2:10 NLT

Our devotion to God leads us to be more devoted to others. That's because God's Spirit is at work in us, encouraging us to do what's right. When we keep our promises, weigh our words, and offer a helping hand with no expectation of reward, we are loving God by loving others. Our faith-filled devotion to God brings out the best in us while, at the same time, blessing those around us.

Lord, forgive me for not living out my devotion to You with actions. Forgive me for my laziness, selfishness, and unkindness. Forgive me for giving to others with any thought to my own profit. May I seek to bless others in all I do, regardless of the cost or the reward. Amen.

Day 239

Flip the Switch

Keep your minds on whatever is true, pure, right, holy, friendly, and proper. Don't ever stop thinking about what is truly worthwhile and worthy of praise.
PHILIPPIANS 4:8 CEV

Some trains of thought need to be derailed. That's because they don't lead you closer to becoming the woman God created you to be. But like a switch operator who changes the track a train is on to save it from disaster, you can change the direction of your thoughts. If others could read your mind and you'd be embarrassed by what they read, flip the switch. Choose to focus on something worthy of your time and God's praise.

Dear Lord, when my mind leads me astray, give me the strength to turn to scripture instead. Help me today—and tomorrow and in the days to come—to fill my thoughts with Your Word so that it is what I meditate upon in unoccupied moments. Amen.

Day 240
Changed Minds

Create pure thoughts in me and make me faithful again.
Psalm 51:10 CEV

Living a life that pleases God is more than doing the right thing. It's also thinking the right thing. That's because faith isn't about appearances. It's about reality. It's about all of you: body, mind, and spirit. This transformation doesn't happen overnight. But the more time you spend with God, the more aware you'll become of random thoughts that don't line up with your faith. Take those thoughts to God. Ask Him to help change your mind for good.

Lord, we put on a good face when behind that smiling mask lurk thoughts too wicked, despair too deep, to say aloud. We long to be transformed. Discipline us for the long work of sanctification. You are in the business of changing sinners from the inside out. Amen.

Day 241

Spiritually Alive

Spiritually alive, we have access to everything God's Spirit is doing, and can't be judged by unspiritual critics. Isaiah's question, "Is there anyone around who knows God's Spirit, anyone who knows what he is doing?" has been answered: Christ knows, and we have Christ's Spirit.

1 CORINTHIANS 2:15–16 MSG

When we have the Spirit of Jesus alive in us, we are being transformed. God's Word is brought to life in us, and we are able to understand things that we couldn't before—we are taught right and wrong. The ancient theologian Augustine said, "Without the Spirit we can neither love God nor keep His commandments." The Holy Spirit helps us to do both!

Jesus, I'm so thankful I don't have to do life on my own. You are giving me the power to accomplish everything You ask of me. Thank You for making me spiritually alive!

Day 242
God at Work

Give thanks in all circumstances; for this is God's will for you in Christ Jesus.
1 THESSALONIANS 5:18 NIV

Faith gives you new eyes, along with a new heart. As you look more consistently in God's direction, you become aware of things you never noticed before: the miraculous detail of God's creation, the countless gifts He gives each day, His answers to prayer, and His persistence in bringing something positive out of even the most negative circumstances. It's good to notice God at work. It's even better to say "thank You" when you do. What will you thank Him for today?

Lord, I thank You for the view outside my window, for the warm clothes I am wearing, for the smell of pancakes from the kitchen, for the voices of my children and husband, for the clink of forks on plates. You are present in this house this morning, and I praise You. Amen.

Day 243

Incomprehensible Peace

Do not be anxious about anything, but in every situation, by prayer and petition, with thanksgiving, present your requests to God. And the peace of God, which transcends all understanding, will guard your hearts and your minds in Christ Jesus.

PHILIPPIANS 4:6–7 NIV

Peace is living out the fact that God is in control and that you belong to Him. The chaos and uncertainty of this world will test your trust in God. But if you own this scripture and live it, His peace will cocoon your mind and heart. In everything, trust Him. In every situation, pray. And peace beyond understanding will comfort you. You may not understand it, and the world will look at you and wonder how you could possibly be at peace, but your mind will rest easy.

Father, I submit to Your control. No matter what happens, You are my God and I belong to You. Amen.

Day 244

Special People

I have not stopped giving thanks for you,
remembering you in my prayers.
EPHESIANS 1:16 NIV

There are many ways of showing gratitude. You can send flowers or share a hug. You can say "thanks" with a note, text, e-mail, or phone call. But have you ever considered expressing your gratitude via prayer? Asking for God's guidance and blessing on those who've generously touched your life with their love takes thankfulness to the next level—an eternal one. It also reminds you to thank God for His gift of bringing these special people into your life.

Dear Father, remind me when my mind wanders to unprofitable places that I need to pray instead. Bring people to my mind who have touched my life in eternal ways. Thankfulness brings me joy and reminds me how You have been faithful to me through other believers. Amen.

Day 245

Transformed Doubts

The father instantly cried out, "I do believe, but help me overcome my unbelief!"
MARK 9:24 NLT

Entrusting friends and family to God's care isn't always easy. One reason is that as women, we're born caretakers—and we doubt anyone can care for those we love as well as we do. Faith assures us that God is the only perfect caregiver. When we worry about someone, we're doubting God's love, power, and plan for that person's life. Bring every doubt and worry to God in prayer. Then allow Him to transform your doubts into faith.

Dear Lord, You know how my faith rises and falls like the waves of the sea. Sometimes I trust, but more often I try to soldier on under my own power. Forgive me for trying to carry the burdens that only You can. Help me to give those burdens back to You. Amen.

Day 246

Feeling Lonely

"For whoever does the will of my Father in heaven is my brother and sister and mother."
MATTHEW 12:50 ESV

Family is important to Jesus. Psalm 68:6 (NIV) tells us that "God sets the lonely in families." He made us to be in a community with other people. We learn from each other and grow and share God's love when we live in relationships with other people. God doesn't want us to be lonely. You are a child of God, so that means you are part of God's family! If you are having a hard time finding good friends right now, ask Jesus for help! He cares about your relationships and wants you to have the family of God around you to help you in this life.

Jesus, will You help me to find other believers who love You and want to follow You? Please show me what it means to be a part of Your family.

Day 247

Diligent Overseer

For we are God's handiwork, created in Christ Jesus to do good works, which God prepared in advance for us to do.
EPHESIANS 2:10 NIV

God has given us so many wonderful gifts. And everything we have—money, time, abilities—ultimately belongs to God. We're just overseers of His abundant wealth. Following Christ doesn't mean that we laze through life waiting for Jesus to return and take us on an eternal vacation. Instead, Jesus calls us to be about our Father's business, just as He was. How will Jesus find the resources He has entrusted to you when He returns? Will He find them wasted or neglected, or will He ecstatically discover that you've put them to good use for His glory?

Father, show me the untapped resources I have at my disposal and enable me to use them to honor You. When I see You face-to-face, I long to hear, "Well done." Amen.

Day 248

Consistent Effort

"The market is flooded with surefire, easygoing formulas for a successful life. . . . The way to life—to God!—is vigorous and requires total attention."

MATTHEW 7:13–14 MSG

Some people confuse luck with success. They want the reward of a successful life without having to put in the work. But success is something that's achieved over time. Whether it's in the workplace, parenting your children, or growing in your faith, success is the result of consistent effort toward reaching a goal. A successful life is made up of successful days—and a truly successful day is one that draws you closer to God and His plans for you.

Dear Lord, when we think of a life in which success is defined in Your terms, we need think no further than Paul. He gave up a high position as a Pharisee to be imprisoned, shipwrecked, and reviled for following You. Give us the faith to go and do likewise. Amen.

Day 249

Erased!

When you ask for something, you must have faith and not doubt. Anyone who doubts is like an ocean wave tossed around in a storm.

James 1:6 CEV

You wouldn't ask a gardener to trim your hair or a house painter to paint your nails. When you ask someone to do something, you ask only those who you believe can actually do what needs to be done. God can do anything that's in line with His will. If you pray without expecting God to answer, doubt is derailing your faith. Ask God to help you understand the "whys" behind your doubts. He can help you erase each one.

Dear God, when we truly understand Your power and love, we will no longer doubt. You can do anything! Help us to pray in faith, knowing You are always hearing and answering, even if sometimes Your answer is "no" or "not yet." We rest in that. Amen.

Day 250
Rejection

Then Jesus asked them, "Didn't you ever read this in the Scriptures? 'The stone that the builders rejected has now become the cornerstone. This is the LORD's doing, and it is wonderful to see.'"

MATTHEW 21:42 NLT

Jesus knows exactly what it feels like to be rejected. During His earthly ministry, many people followed Him, but in the end, the religious leaders turned people against Him and sent Him to die on a cross. Even some of His friends betrayed Him. The crowds called for Jesus to be crucified. They humiliated him. But He endured all of the mental, emotional, and physical anguish out of His deep love for us. People rejected Jesus, but God had chosen Him. Remember this the next time you feel alone or forgotten. God chose you to be His much-loved child. Jesus sees everything that is happening to you, and He understands your heart. He is with you.

Jesus, thank You for all that You endured on my behalf. Your love is astounding.

Day 251

God Knows What He's Doing

I'll show up and take care of you as I promised and bring you back home. I know what I'm doing. I have it all planned out—plans to take care of you, not abandon you, plans to give you the future you hope for.
JEREMIAH 29:11 MSG

God wants good to come to you. He wants you to find Him and know Him personally. He wants you to know that you are never alone and that you always have access to the greatest power in the world. That's good news! Psalm 31:19 (GNT) says, "How wonderful are the good things you keep for those who honor you! Everyone knows how good you are, how securely you protect those who trust you." Following Jesus is the most important decision you can ever make. He has good plans for your life.

Jesus, I trust You with my life.

Day 252

In Line with God's Goals

Commit to the L*ORD whatever you do,*
and he will establish your plans.
PROVERBS 16:3 NIV

Faith's definition of *success* differs from that of the world. Whereas our culture applauds people of fame, wealth, and power, faith regards those who live their lives according to God's purpose as successful. Committing whatever you do to God isn't asking Him to bless what you've already decided to do. It's inviting Him into the planning process. Make sure your dreams and goals are in line with God's. Then get to work—leaving the end result in His hands.

Thank You, Lord, that Your plans are to prosper me. But often I miss the most important part of that verse: it says Your plans. Not mine. In order to succeed, my plans need to be Your plans. Give me the wisdom to see where You are leading and the faith to follow. Amen.

Day 253

Made Right

For all men have sinned and have missed the shining-greatness of God. Anyone can be made right with God by the free gift of His loving-favor. It is Jesus Christ Who bought them with His blood and made them free from their sins.

ROMANS 3:23–24 NLV

We all mess up, sometimes worse than others. But the main point is not the degree of our sin, but rather the fact that we do sin—all of us. And while we can't get a do-over, friend, there's hope. Jesus lived a perfect life and then died in your place—and mine. We're free. Forgiven. When we confess our sins and accept His forgiveness, we step into the boundless grace of our great and loving God.

Father, I'm so sorry for the wrong I've done against You. The depth of Your love takes my breath away—that You would die for me. Amen.

Day 254

The Wisdom of Silence

A fool always loses his temper, but a wise man keeps quiet.
PROVERBS 29:11 NLV

We all get upset sometimes. But it's how you react that will showcase your wisdom—or prove you a fool. Our heavenly Father says that wisdom is using your self-control, even when you're angry. Keeping a tight rein on your control is even more important when you're upset. After all, it's not much of a show of control when you have nothing to be aggravated about. Too often anger drives us into sin—yelling, slamming doors, using hurtful words, and engaging in various kinds of abuse. The next time you feel your ire rising, stop and pray. Ask God to bolster your self-control.

Father, give me strength. Keep me from saying or doing hurtful things in anger. Amen.

Day 255

Growing Friendship and Faith

When we get together, I want to encourage you in your faith, but I also want to be encouraged by yours.

Romans 1:12 NLT

When women get together, there's usually a whole lot of talking going on. Conversing, counseling, giggling, and catching up on the latest news are all wonderful ways to build a friendship. But if you want to build your faith, take time to encourage one another. Tell your friends how you've seen God at work in their lives. Share what God's been teaching you. Ask questions. Pray. Praise. Your friendship will grow right along with your faith.

Dear gracious heavenly Father, thank You so much for my friends. They are truly gifts from You and bring me strength, joy, and wisdom in abundance. Help me to cherish them. Help our friendship to be firmly rooted in Christ so that together we may grow closer to You. Amen.

Day 256

You've Got This

Guard the good deposit that was entrusted to you—
guard it with the help of the Holy Spirit who lives in us.
2 TIMOTHY 1:14 NIV

The Message says it this way: "So keep at your work, this faith and love rooted in Christ, exactly as I set it out for you. It's as sound as the day you first heard it from me. Guard this precious thing placed in your custody by the Holy Spirit who works in us." As a child of God, chosen before the foundation of the world, you've been given a special gift to guard and protect: the truth of God's saving Word. You don't have to guard this on your own, for you have the Spirit's power alive inside you. This knowledge should give you rest, not intimidation. You've got this—because He's got you!

Lord, I'm truly beginning to see that I have nothing to worry about. Your power is at work in me always.

Day 257

The Helper

"But the Helper (Comforter, Advocate, Intercessor— Counselor, Strengthener, Standby), the Holy Spirit, whom the Father will send in My name [in My place, to represent Me and act on My behalf], He will teach you all things. And He will help you remember everything that I have told you."

JOHN 14:26 AMP

The Holy Spirit is our counselor, teacher, comforter, and guide—the promise that we are never alone fulfilled! The Spirit is the power of God alive inside of everyone who believes and commits to following Jesus. Through His power, we have everything we need (2 Peter 1:3). When we don't know what to do, we can ask! When we don't know what to pray, the Spirit helps (Romans 8:26)!

Come, Holy Spirit. Fill my heart with Your presence and peace. Thank You for helping me in everything and in every way.

Day 258

A Second Wind

Strength is for service, not status. Each one of us needs to look after the good of the people around us, asking ourselves, "How can I help?"

ROMANS 15:1 MSG

When you're feeling worn out, it's hard to think about meeting anyone's needs other than your own. But sometimes that's exactly what God asks you to do. Perhaps it's your children who need your help in the middle of the night. Or maybe it's a stranger whose car has broken down by the side of the road. When God nudges you to respond, call on Him for strength. His Spirit will rouse your compassion, providing you with a second wind.

Lord, I am tired today, but I know You have put me in a place where I can serve the needs of many. Help me to put aside how I feel, to rely on Your strength, and to rejoice that You supply my every need so I can meet the needs of others. Amen.

Day 259

Hope in Him

Why, my soul, are you downcast? Why so disturbed within me? Put your hope in God, for I will yet praise him, my Savior and my God.

PSALM 42:5 NIV

Does your future look brighter if you have a hefty bank account or a prestigious position or do loads of charity work? Or maybe hope for the future sparks with a new relationship. When things are going well, these things can seem to sustain our good mood, but do they offer hope when friends betray you or your health fails or your loved ones die? Don't be fooled into propping your future against failing supports. Put your hope in God—the only one who will never fail you—and see how He can transform certain despair into hope of a good future.

Father, I have no cause to be disturbed when I put my hope in You. When I'm feeling low, remind me to faithfully trust in Your plan. Amen.

Day 260

Why Do You Contend with Me?

"I will say to God, 'Don't simply not condemn me—
tell me the charge you are bringing against me.'"
JOB 10:2 NLT

Tough love—sometimes as parents we use hard measures against our children to equip them for the future, to teach them a better way. It doesn't mean we're unsympathetic or unfeeling. On the contrary, our great love compels us to prepare them fully for the future. And if we can employ such designs with our children, how much more can God's great love move Him to teach us maturity! As believers we sometimes cry out with Job in the midst of struggles, "Why are You striving against me?" Whether you've been through something or are going through something now, how is God using hard things to hone your faith?

Heavenly Father, I know You love me.
Teach me to grow stronger through my struggles. Amen.

Day 261

You're Loved

The humble will see their God at work and be glad.
Let all who seek God's help be encouraged.
PSALM 69:32 NLT

Asking someone for help can be humbling, even if that someone is a close girlfriend. But if she agrees to assist you and actually comes through for you, you can't help but be encouraged. Knowing someone reached out to you means that person cares. It means you matter. You're loved. Know that God's help means the very same thing. He cares for you because He cares *about* you. Let that fact encourage you in your faith today.

Lord, thank You for our friends who have acted as the hands and feet of Jesus. They are Your instruments in our lives, and we praise You for Your care of us through their ministry. Help us to ask for help as easily as we give it. Amen.

Day 262

Beautiful Things

Do your best to improve your faith by adding goodness, understanding, self-control, patience, devotion to God, concern for others, and love.

2 PETER 1:5–7 CEV

Only God can make a seed grow. But you can make conditions favorable to help that seed mature and bear fruit. The same is true with faith. Cultivate the seed of faith God has planted in you through obedience. When God reveals a weed budding in your character, pull it up by the roots. A fresh sprout of love? Water it regularly with kindness and sacrifice. Tend to your spiritual growth each day and beautiful things will begin to take root.

Lord, You long for us to grow and flourish. You aren't content to keep us small and weak in the faith. You send struggles—winds and droughts—that cause us to grow stronger and send our roots down deeper in You. Thank You for tending us with so much care. Amen.

Day 263

Step-by-Step

I can do everything through Christ, who gives me strength.
PHILIPPIANS 4:13 NLT

Picture yourself in a race, struggling to reach the finish line. You're exhausted, discouraged, perhaps even injured. You're tempted to give up. Then a friend runs onto the course from the sidelines. She places her arm around your waist, inviting you to lean on her for strength and support. Together, step-by-step, you see the race to completion. God is that kind of friend. Whether the strength you need today is physical, emotional, or spiritual, God is there. Lean on Him.

Father, thank You for coming alongside me when I am weary. I feel Your comfort and strength flow into me as I meditate on Your Word, when I pray, and when I gather to speak of You with other believers. Thank You for meeting me right here in my weakness. Amen.

Day 264

Path to Heaven

God loved the people of this world so much that he gave his only Son, so that everyone who has faith in him will have eternal life and never really die.

JOHN 3:16 CEV

Eternal life doesn't begin after you die. It begins the day you put your faith in Jesus' love. Right now, you're in the childhood of eternity. You're learning and growing. Like a toddler trying to master the art of walking, you may wobble a bit at times. But if you fall, God helps get you back on your feet again. Once your faith sets you on the path toward heaven, nothing—absolutely nothing—can prevent you from reaching your destination.

Dear Father in heaven, help keep us walking forward, toward You, until our faith eventually becomes sight in eternity. Forgive us for our wobbles, missteps, and wrong turns. Thank You for helping to keep our eyes fixed on You and the sure promise of eternal life. Amen.

Day 265

God Is Faithful

God has said, "I will never leave you or let you be alone."
HEBREWS 13:5 NLV

No one is completely faithful all the time—that is, except Jesus. Humans are just that—human. We mess up. We make mistakes. We get things wrong sometimes. But God never does. He is faithful all the time! And He directs all His love and faithfulness toward you. He'll never forget you. He'll never give up on you. He'll never lie to you. He'll never ever stop loving you. Nothing you could ever do will change His mind about how much He loves you. God looks at you and smiles because He sees Jesus in you. You are covered in His righteousness (2 Corinthians 5:21).

God, I'm so thankful that I'm always on Your mind and that You always keep Your promises to me.

Day 266

Always

"Teach them to do all the things I have told you. And I am with you always, even to the end of the world."

MATTHEW 28:20 NLV

After Jesus conquered death and rose from the grave, He appeared many times to His followers. The last thing He had to say to them and to us before He went back to heaven is this: "I am with you always." The last thing someone says to you is usually pretty important. And this is the most important thing God wanted us to know. He is Immanuel, God with us. Always. His Spirit is alive in our hearts. Any confidence we have is flimsy at best unless it is based on the knowledge that the Spirit of Christ is alive and at work within us!

Jesus, thank You for Your great love for me. Overwhelm me with the truth that You are always with me.

Day 267

Training Ground of Trials

He trains my hands for battle; he strengthens my arm to draw a bronze bow.

Psalm 18:34 NLT

The grueling exercises of boot camp churn out mature, highly disciplined, and fully capable soldiers. Charles Spurgeon wrote, "See you not, then, that God may take away your comforts and your privileges to make you the better Christians? Why, the Lord always trains his soldiers, not by letting them lie on feather beds, but by turning them out and using them to forced marches and hard service. He makes them ford through streams, and swim through rivers, and climb mountains, and walk many a long march with heavy knapsacks of sorrow on their backs. . . . Warriors are really educated by the smell of powder, in the midst of whizzing bullets, and roaring cannonades—not in soft and peaceful times."

Heavenly Father, hone me into a mature, disciplined, and capable warrior. Amen.

Day 268

Why Do We Train?

Be alert and of sober mind. Your enemy the devil prowls around like a roaring lion looking for someone to devour.

1 PETER 5:8 NIV

Maybe you have zero desire to bend a bow of bronze like David, but God has your protection and victory in mind when He hones your spiritual muscles by allowing you to struggle. If you want to build muscle, you pump some iron. Likewise, spiritual strength and understanding grow by grappling with God's truth. God knows these survival skills are vital to your faith because the enemy lurks in the darkness, seeking to take you down. What attacks are devouring you—doubt, fear, discontent, unforgiveness, anger? Pull out your Bible and find scripture you can use to fight back.

Father, keep me alert to Satan's attacks. Prepare my mind with Your words of truth and give me victory. Amen.

Day 269

A Happy Ending

Because you kept on believing, you'll get what you're looking forward to: total salvation.
1 PETER 1:9 MSG

Your salvation comes through faith in Christ. The end result of that salvation is eternal life. Though you're not home in heaven yet, that doesn't mean its existence isn't relevant to you right now. Holding on to your hope of heaven gives you an eternal perspective. It frees you from the fear of death, inspires you to tell others about God's everlasting love, and reminds you that no matter what you face in this life, you're guaranteed a happy ending.

Lord, You are so good. Thank You for the gift of salvation that was ours the moment we believed! That present reality and future hope is a gift You offer to everyone, and we pray that You would give us the strength and courage to share that gift with others. Amen.

Day 270

Praise in the Routine

From the rising of the sun to the going down of it and from east to west, the name of the Lord is to be praised!

Psalm 113:3 AMPC

Those who research such things tell us that routines are good and healthy. Yet they can be boring; sometimes we dread them.

Keeping hope alive every day in the middle of our never-ending routines is a challenge. But the psalmist found something that aided his ability to focus on what is most important—worship. Even our daily routines can be acts of worship. Worship is, after all, giving reverence and adoration to God. As we complete our daily tasks in ways that honor His Word, we may count it as a kind of worship.

Father God, today in my routine, I find hope as I give You praise. Thank You for providing for me and being the energy in my day. Amen.

Day 271

Immanuel

"The virgin will conceive and give birth to a son, and they will call him Immanuel" (which means "God with us").
MATTHEW 1:23 NIV

The baby born long ago in a stable, the Son of the living God, is our Immanuel, God with us. God literally took human form and walked among us, and then He sent us the Holy Spirit so we'd never be without Him. Peace is not the absence of trouble but the presence of God in the midst of trouble. When you face a raging storm, or maybe you're already hit with gale-force winds—whether it's difficult relationships, job loss, health problems, or anxiety—God is with you. The source of your peace will never leave you.

Immanuel, thank You for the comfort and peace of mind I have in knowing that You are here with me. Amen.

Day 272

Letting Go

Understand this, my dear brothers and sisters: You must all be quick to listen, slow to speak, and slow to get angry. Human anger does not produce the righteousness God desires.

JAMES 1:19–20 NLT

Your friend's insensitive words play on a loop in your brain long after the party has ended. By the next morning, not only are you cranky from sleep deprivation but you're also ready to hand her a piece of your mind. Maybe what she said wasn't true, or maybe it was; either way, it hurt. But holding on to your anger damages you more than her piercing words. Forgive, move on, and overlook this offense, because your anger won't lead you to love like Jesus. And you've probably said a few hurtful things you'd like overlooked too.

Father, give me a readily forgiving heart.
Help me to stop angry thoughts before they grow. Amen.

Day 273

Powerful Lessons

Teach believers with your life: by word, by demeanor, by love, by faith, by integrity.
1 TIMOTHY 4:12 MSG

As a little girl, perhaps you played "school" before you ever attended class. If you had the coveted role of "teacher," you got to tell your friends what to do. As an adult, you're still playing the role of teacher, whether you're aware of it or not. When what you believe changes the way you live and love, others notice. Who knows? The most powerful lessons you ever teach may be those in which you never say a word.

Lord, without speaking the Word, my demeanor, love, faith, and integrity often just make others think I'm a "good person." Help me to show them, instead, that I am a sinner saved only by grace. Only You are good! Praise the Lord! Amen.

Day 274

A Good Friend

A friend loves at all times, and a brother is born for a time of adversity.
PROVERBS 17:17 NIV

Sometimes we feel less than loving toward our friends. Maybe they've hurt our feelings or we're too wrapped up in our own busyness to listen to their troubles. Good friends are hard to find, and being a good friend to others can be equally difficult. But sometimes we need help through the struggles of life—and that's where friends come in. Take a moment and think of a friend you have who is trustworthy, kind, and dependable, and thank God for putting her in your life. And if you can't bring to mind a single person, ask God for a friend. He'd love to oblige.

Father, thank You for giving me friends that I can count on. Help me to be a good friend in return. Show me how I can help and encourage them in hard times. Amen.

Day 275

Unburdened

"Be careful, or your hearts will be weighed down with. . .the anxieties of life."
LUKE 21:34 NIV

Have you ever felt overwhelmed? Of course you have, friend, because at some point in this messy journey, we all do. Jesus doesn't expect us not to experience the stresses of life. He knows that our enemy prowls around like a hungry lion looking for ways to devour our peace. No, having problems isn't really our issue when we're overtaken by anxiety. It's how we react. Some of us get snappy, some of us cry, and some of us hide. Jesus longs for you to come and sit at His feet and lay down those heavy burdens of life, knowing that He can provide.

Jesus, help me to trust You to provide in every circumstance. You have the answers, wisdom, and resources I need. Amen.

Day 276

Laugh and Be Strong

"For the joy of the Lord is your strength."
Nehemiah 8:10 ESV

A laughing woman is stronger than a sullen one.

To look at everyday life and find something to laugh about takes a strong woman. And the action of laughter generates more strength. Laughing releases good endorphins and helps us process life in a positive way. No, we don't laugh about bad things; we laugh in spite of them.

We don't know if Jesus laughed a lot, but it's not out of character to think He did. Hebrews 12:2 tells us that He endured the cross for future joy. If we endure, by His grace, we will share eternity with Him. And in the meantime, we can laugh.

Father God, thank You for creating me with the ability to laugh. Help me to access this powerful tool today for Your glory and my good. Amen.

Day 277

Keeping Sane

You keep him in perfect peace whose mind is stayed on you, because he trusts in you.
ISAIAH 26:3 ESV

We can feel fractured in mind and emotion on certain days because of a crammed schedule or personal physical difficulties or relational challenges or a combination of all of it.

We are not promised that life will be, as our grandmothers used to say, "a bed of roses." Being a follower of Christ does not guarantee ease and comfort, but it does give us assurance that He is with us in every moment. The ancient prophet was inspired to write these empowering words—He will keep us in peace if we focus our thoughts on Him. When you are tempted to zero in on still another problem, meet the thought with the confidence that Christ will be there to help you solve it.

Lord, today I focus my thoughts and my mental responses on Your sufficiency. Thank You for giving me peace. Amen.

Day 278

The Meaning of Love

You obey the whole Law when you do this one thing,
"Love your neighbor as you love yourself."
Galatians 5:14 NLV

In today's world, *love* is a pretty casual word. We love our favorite jeans and we love our children. We love ice cream and we love God. Love often means something that brings pleasure to our lives. But God's picture of love is not self-indulgent. God-love denies itself and gives unconditionally without expecting something in return. Scripture teaches us how to recognize love: it is patient, kind, not envious, boastful, or proud. It honors others, is not selfish or easily angered, and keeps no record of wrongs. It doesn't delight in evil, rejoices with the truth, protects, trusts, hopes, and perseveres. Are you ready to take up the challenge of loving others?

Father, may my behavior toward others reflect the perfect love You have for me. Amen.

Day 279

Be Still

"The Lord will fight for you; you need only to be still."
Exodus 14:14 NIV

Tragedy, death, betrayal, illness, addiction, failure, loss, poverty, abuse—life can wound us horribly. And we find it difficult to trust God when it seems as if He is not paying attention to the collapse of our world. But friend, the thought that God can't, won't, or doesn't care to step into your circumstances is a poisonous lie of the enemy, put into your mind to weaken your faith. When all seems lost, trust. When hope fades, trust. Sometimes the hardest task is not what God asks you to do but what He asks you not to do. Don't trust in your own plans. The Lord will fight for you.

Father, I know that You love me beyond compare. Sometimes I feel the need to fix things when I really should be praying and trusting. Amen.

Day 280

Pardoned!

Who is a God like you, who pardons sin?
MICAH 7:18 NIV

"Will you forgive me?" Never have any other words burgeoned with such tentative hope. We desire to have our shame wiped away and our wrongdoing passed over. One of the first things we're introduced to in the Bible is the shame and punishment linked to human sin. But oh, beloved daughter, this isn't the end of God's story. Hope pierces the darkness with scouring light because we serve a God who pardons sin. His grace covers our shame. Have you experienced the freeing soul-relief of forgiveness? It's yours for the asking. "If we confess our sins, he is faithful and just to forgive us our sins and to cleanse us from all unrighteousness" (1 John 1:9 ESV).

Father, I know I've sinned. Please forgive me and strengthen me to choose right. Joy washes through me because of Your mercy. Amen.

Day 281

Your Choice

"Choose for yourselves this day whom you will serve. . . .
But as for me and my household, we will serve the Lord."
Joshua 24:15 NIV

We make a thousand choices every day. Most mean little in the long run, but the rest of our lives and even our eternities hinge on what we choose—who our friends are, what we do with our time and resources. What will we eat, watch on television, or listen to? Will we use kind words or rude? Will we pray and read scripture today or choose a novel instead? Our character is built from the bricks of our everyday choices. Take a moment and inventory your choices this week. Who are you serving with the decisions you've made? Are you serving God with righteous living?

Father, reveal the choices I'm
making that don't honor You. Amen.

Day 282

He Hears My Voice!

I love the Lord, because He hears my voice and my prayers.
Psalm 116:1 NLV

Your friend's voice drones into the background of your thoughts, and you realize you missed half her story. We're not always the best listeners. But thankfully, our heavenly Father doesn't suffer from our shortcoming. He is never distracted or uninterested in what we have to say to Him. He hears our prayers. In a world of lonely, disconnected people, we kindle a blaze of hope by sharing the news that there's no time or place that we cannot have a conversation with the great God who created us and loves us. It's beyond amazing that we have this kind of unlimited access to the living God.

God, I'm in awe that You, Creator of the universe, listen to my problems and take the time to speak to me. Thank You for Your boundless love for me. Amen.

Day 283

One Worth Following

Follow the example of the correct teaching I gave you,
and let the faith and love of Christ Jesus be your model.
2 TIMOTHY 1:13 CEV

The Bible's a pretty thick book. It looks like there's a lot to learn. But Jesus said that if we love God and others, we've fulfilled everything written there. How do we do that? Look to Jesus' own life as recorded in the gospels. Jesus never treats people like an interruption or inconvenience. He listens, comforts, and cares. He spends time with His Father in prayer, regardless of His busy schedule. Jesus' example is one worth following.

Dear Lord, one of the miracles of the Christian life is that it's simple enough for a child to come to faith yet complex enough to keep us thinking, praying, and praising our entire lives. Help us to reach out to others with the simple, rich message of the gospel. Amen.

Day 284

The Good Old Life

Older women likewise are to be reverent in behavior, not slanderers or slaves to much wine. They are to teach what is good.

TITUS 2:3 ESV

Have you ever met a woman who was excited about aging? Generally, it's not something we welcome.

But the apostle Paul was divinely inspired to write about older women in his letter to Titus. They are to have good behavior, not spending their time gossiping or drinking (that flies in the face of the retired, living-on-the-golf-course-with-a-glass-of-wine mentality!). And get this: they are to teach good things. One version says, "They should be examples of the good life" (PHILLIPS). Don't you love that? Following God's blueprint gives older women a good life to model for younger women. Talk about strength in aging. That's it!

God, You give me strength in every life season. Thank You for this good life. Amen.

Day 285

Victory over Death

You have been given a new birth. It was from a seed that cannot die. This new life is from the Word of God which lives forever. All people are like grass. Their greatness is like the flowers. The grass dries up and the flowers fall off. But the Word of the Lord will last forever.

1 PETER 1:23–25 NLV

Fatal car accidents, unexpected illnesses, tragic crimes—people are dying all around us. And to stave off panic over the transient nature of life, we numb ourselves to their passing. Scripture says that human lives wither like the grass, here one moment and gone the next—but remember God's promise! This world is just the prelude. Through Christ, we are born from an eternal seed into new, everlasting life. If you fear death, accept His gift of eternal life. And if you already have, maybe you've lost sight of just how much God loves you.

God, I look forward to eternity with hopeful expectation. Amen.

Day 286

Forgive

A man's understanding makes him slow to anger.
It is to his honor to forgive and forget a wrong done to him.
PROVERBS 19:11 NLV

Forgiveness can be hard work. When someone injures us, often anger floods in. We know scripture says to forgive, but we're suffering emotionally. In this moment be very careful not to let the enemy get the upper hand and convince you that you're justified in holding a grudge. The truth is that forgiveness doesn't mean that what was done against you was right or okay; instead, it means that you choose not to sin in your suffering. Jesus, who had far more right to feel justified, said, "Father, forgive them," as they nailed Him to the cross. Are you harboring any offenses today?

Father, help me to let go of grudges. I don't want to allow bitterness and anger to twine roots into my soul. Amen.

Day 287

On the Run

Where can I go from your Spirit?
Where can I flee from your presence?
Psalm 139:7 NIV

Have you ever wanted to hide from your mistakes? When our anger gets the best of us and we snap at our children, when we shade the truth to look better for our friends, we feel the pinch of the Holy Spirit's chiding in our soul—and we sometimes make haste to hide from the Father. But sweet daughter, God already knows. There's nowhere we can run from Him and no hiding from His Spirit. But there's comfort here in this truth as well. No matter how far out of bounds we think we've strayed, the grace and love of the Father can catch us even there. Have you been afraid to face God in the aftermath of your failure? Rest assured, His grace is sufficient.

Father, I'm sorry for hiding from You.
Please forgive me. Amen.

Day 288

Healing Joy

A joyful heart is good medicine,
but a crushed spirit dries up the bones.
PROVERBS 17:22 ESV

Joy in your heart can change your perspective of even desperate circumstances. Paul and Silas showed us that even after being beaten and thrown in prison, they could still choose joy in their salvation and even sing praises to God through bruised and broken bodies. Your attitude can really influence your outlook. Next time you're feeling battered by life, choose joy anyway and see how it brightens your spirits. We have a heavenly Father who adores us and eternity in heaven awaiting! The world is watching. And just as Paul and Silas led the jailer and his household to Jesus (Acts 16), your joy can bring others to Christ.

Father, help me to choose joy instead of depression today. I don't want to wallow in a negative perspective. I have a song in my heart because I trust in You. Amen.

Day 289

A Glimpse of God

In the morning, Lord, you hear my voice; in the morning I lay my requests before you and wait expectantly.

Psalm 5:3 NIV

If you're expecting an important package, you're often on the lookout for the mail carrier. You peek out the window. Listen for footsteps. Check the mailbox. When you pray, are you on the lookout for God's answers? Not every answer will be delivered when, where, and how you expect. So keep your eyes open and your heart expectant. Don't miss out on the joy of catching a glimpse of God at work.

Dear Lord, thank You for the reminder in the psalms that You hear my voice. I am known by You and loved—so I can wait patiently and be certain that You will answer in the way that is best for me. What assurance! What peace! In praise and thanksgiving, amen.

Day 290

No Guarantees Except His Arms

"The eternal God is your refuge, and his everlasting arms are under you. He drives out the enemy before you; he cries out, 'Destroy them!' "
DEUTERONOMY 33:27 NLT

Guarantees are a wonderful thing. Sears, Roebuck and Company, started in the late 1890s by Richard W. Sears and Alvah C. Roebuck, was a name synonymous with the "money-back guarantee" for much of the twentieth century. People liked that they could change their mind and be assured they wouldn't lose their investment.

As Christians, we have no guarantees of easy living or a hefty bank account or protection from hardship. We are subject to all the ills of our fallen world just like anyone else. But we do have the guarantee of His presence as our constant refuge. There is no situation on earth in which He cannot bring good in the end. And even Sears couldn't promise that.

Heavenly Father, thank You for the promise of Your arms of strength around me in any situation. Amen.

Day 291

Even If He Doesn't

"The God we serve is able to deliver us from it, and he will deliver us from Your Majesty's hand. But even if he does not, we want you to know, Your Majesty, that we will not serve your gods or worship the image of gold you have set up."

DANIEL 3:17–18 NIV

When life goes horribly wrong, we cry out for escape. Our first thought, and often desperate prayer, is "Please, get me out of here!" Shadrach, Meshach, and Abednego didn't back down from their faith. They braved the fire—and walked out of the furnace without a hint of smoke on their clothes. But they were prepared to trust God. They knew He *could* deliver them even if He didn't. What potential setbacks do you face? Are you willing to trust God even if things don't come out as you planned?

Father, I trust that Your plan is good.
My faith is in You no matter what. Amen.

Day 292

A Father's Broken Heart

And do not bring sorrow to God's Holy Spirit by the way you live.
EPHESIANS 4:30 NLT

Our children can pierce our hearts with pain. With the power of a few wrong choices, they bring us to our knees. And hopefully, we're praying from this position. But this heartbreak is a mere reflection of the sorrow we bring to God's heart with the sin we often embrace. Each moment of gossip, each angry word or selfish act—each sin is a turn of the knife. Just as we want better for our offspring than a lifetime of regret and poor choices that lead to endless suffering, God wants more for us too. He wants us to run and not grow weary. He wants us to soar. How have your actions grieved your Father recently?

Lord, I'm so sorry I've caused You pain. Show me how I'm hurting You. Help me to choose right. Amen.

Day 293

Grow

Let us move beyond the elementary teachings about Christ and be taken forward to maturity.
HEBREWS 6:1 NIV

Growing pains have earned their name for a reason. Change can hurt. Our kids labor through years of instruction in their schooling. As their brains develop, they can understand more complex ideas and begin to practice problem-solving and decision-making skills. The writer of Hebrews warns that as followers of Christ, we can't stay in elementary school either. We need to move forward into maturity. A fully developed love that acts as Jesus would and a mature recognition of the evil we battle should blossom as we grow up in our faith. Study the Bible and pray about the areas in your life where your growth has stagnated.

Father, give me strength to choose right. Fill me with a desire to know more of Your ways as I grow in maturity. Amen.

Day 294
The Unexpected

Jesus replied, "Why do you say 'if you can'? Anything is possible for someone who has faith!"
MARK 9:23 CEV

What can we expect from God? The unexpected. Many people who came to Jesus asked to be healed. But how Jesus healed them was never the same. He put mud on a blind man's eyes. A bleeding woman merely touched His robe. Sometimes Jesus only spoke—and healing happened. Coming to God in faith means you can expect that He will act. He promises He'll respond to your prayers. How? Anticipate the unexpected.

Lord, I am so glad that You are a living, active God. You're not a genie compelled to appear when the lamp is rubbed; You're not a heavenly slot machine that spills out answers at random. You are always listening, always loving, and always answering. Amen.

Day 295

Unchanging, Ever Faithful

"For I the LORD do not change."
MALACHI 3:6 ESV

Jesus Christ is the same yesterday and today and forever.
HEBREWS 13:8 ESV

You will change [the heavens] like a robe, and they will pass away, but you are the same, and your years have no end.
PSALM 102:26–27 ESV

The greatest source of strength for the woman who loves God is the fact that she can trust in His unchangeability. Humans change, nature changes, cultures and societies change, but He does not. He dwells outside of time and change. He is constantly the same, eternally always. He will be the same tomorrow as today and the same next week as He was last year. We can put our confidence in that and find hope for all our *nevertheless* moments.

O Lord, I praise You because You are unchanging and ever faithful. Keep me centered today. In Jesus' name, amen.

Day 296

Others First

To the humble he gives favor.
Proverbs 3:34 esv

Is the word *humble* stamped across the image of a doormat in your mind—something others scrape their shoes on? Mostly, we'd rather be enthralled with our own importance. As women, we find countless ways to compare ourselves to others. We value ourselves in pounds on a scale, carats in our diamonds, and even the success of our children. Our vanity is boundless as we compete for first place in trivial things. The apostle Paul urged believers to "do nothing out of selfish ambition or vain conceit. Rather, in humility value others above yourselves" (Philippians 2:3 niv). Value others above yourself—just like Jesus did. Who have you been putting first?

Father, teach me to give more value to others. "Me first" is an easy motto to live by. Teach me to consider the needs of others. Amen.

Day 297

A Place for You

"Do not let your hearts be troubled. You believe in God; believe also in me. My Father's house has many rooms; if that were not so, would I have told you that I am going there to prepare a place for you? And if I go and prepare a place for you, I will come back and take you to be with me that you also may be where I am."

JOHN 14:1–3 NIV

Life can be so disappointing, sometimes devastatingly so. We fail, we fall, and we fumble opportunities. We lose jobs, loved ones, and sometimes our minds. But Jesus left us with a powerful promise. He is coming back for us! We will spend eternity where sadness and sin no longer reign, where fear and pain are forever conquered and goodbye is but a memory.

Jesus, You're preparing a better home for me—the one I've been longing for! Amen.

Day 298

An Act of Heart

Let love and faithfulness never leave you; bind them around your neck, write them on the tablet of your heart.

PROVERBS 3:3 NIV

Dogs are known as "man's best friend." That's because dogs are faithful. They don't hold a grudge or get so preoccupied with their own lives that they forget to greet you at the door. That kind of loyalty comes easy to a dog. But for complex human beings, it takes an act of will and heart. With God's help, you can become a woman who others can depend on. Live out your faith by becoming more faithful.

Dear Lord, we long to be faithful as You are faithful—always having the other person in mind and always working for their good. Only Your Spirit can show us how to do this and empower us—in our weakness—with Your faithfulness. Be our guide and sustainer. Amen.

Day 299

Solar Strengthening

Light is sweet, and it is pleasant for the eyes to see the sun.
ECCLESIASTES 11:7 ESV

The sun was created by God to be a source of strength for us. Early pagan peoples often misguidedly worshipped the sun itself instead of the one who made it. But our Creator spoke the sun into existence for our strengthening—it causes the earth to bloom through the process of photosynthesis; it warms the planet so we can exist; its rays on our heads cause the production of serotonin (the happy hormone) in our bodies. The appearance of the sun each new day reminds us that God is in charge of our world. It reminds us of redemption—God can lighten anything we bring to Him in surrender. And that gives us needed strength.

Lord God, You have made the sun to remind me of You. Today, I ask for Your strength. Amen.

Day 300

Number Your Days

Teach us to realize the brevity of life,
so that we may grow in wisdom.
PSALM 90:12 NLT

As we age, time seems to pass faster and faster. Some days I feel as if I'm watching it flash by outside the window of the bullet train. I'd love to hop off the rails and savor every moment, but the days blur by anyway. Maybe this perception of speeding time as we age is actually a gift from God. The faster time passes, the more we see it as a precious commodity. Fleeting things of earth fade. Treasure this day God has given you. Ask Him what He'd like you to do today.

Father, teach me to number my days. Each day is a gift I can give back to You by living holy. Amen.

Day 301

Fear God

But the love of the Lord remains forever with those who fear him. His salvation extends to the children's children.

Psalm 103:17 NLT

Sometimes we humans get a little too caught up in our own importance. We forget the magnitude of who God is—the all-powerful Creator of every grain of sand on every ocean-kissed beach and sun-scorched desert. Magnificent Maker of billions of stars that sparkle like gems against the backdrop of the universe. Master of waves and weather. Artisan of every atom, originator of tiny organisms, shaper of cells—nothing is too hard for Him or lies outside His reach. This great God cares for You with an unquenchable love. Fearing Him means never forgetting that He is God.

God, You are holy and awesome—worthy of my respect and obedience. Thank You for Your love and faithfulness. Amen.

Day 302

The Peace He Gives

"I will ask the Father, and he will give you another advocate to help you and be with you forever—the Spirit of truth. The world cannot accept him, because it neither sees him nor knows him. But you know him, for he lives with you and will be in you. I will not leave you as orphans; I will come to you."

JOHN 14:16–18 NIV

When Jesus left the earth, He asked the Father to send us an incredible gift—our Advocate, Helper, Teacher, Guide, and Comforter—the blessed Holy Spirit who give us peace. "Peace I leave with you; my peace I give you. I do not give to you as the world gives. Do not let your hearts be troubled and do not be afraid" (John 14:27 NIV). The Spirit of God dwells in us.

Father, thank You for the presence, power, and peace of the Holy Spirit in my life. Amen.

Day 303

His Holy Nature Is Our Strength

Your decrees are very trustworthy; holiness befits your house, O Lord, forevermore.

Psalm 93:5 esv

Holiness is a frightening term to some. It seems to signify a rigid and aloof character, an exacting manner that angrily tosses out anyone who isn't a Goody-two-shoes.

Actually, holiness is the most important attribute of our God. If He were not perfectly holy, He would not love us as He does. Because there is no guile or imperfection in Him, He is compassionate and longsuffering, even as He does not lower His standards in compromise. If He were not totally holy, we would wonder if He were being capricious or malicious or disingenuous when bad things happen to us. But we can trust His actions because we can trust His nature.

Lord God, thank You for being holy in all You do and are. I trust You. Amen.

Day 304

Love Wins!

Love never fails.

1 CORINTHIANS 13:8 NIV

It's nearly impossible to find a sure thing. We put our trust in friends who walk away, jobs that disappoint, and possessions that rust and break. But scripture tells of one sure thing that never fails—love. You might say that love has failed you through divorce or betrayal. And it's true: the "love" of humans will falter. But there's one whose love is patient and kind, never jealous or proud. It's never self-seeking or easily angered. His love doesn't keep a record of your offenses. It always protects, trusts, and hopes, and forever will persevere. The love of God never fails. He didn't have to give up His Son to pull us back from death's cold grip, but He did. Love compelled Him. What will your love compel you to do today?

Father, Your love triumphs!
Quicken this same love in my heart. Amen.

Day 305

Adopted

The Spirit himself testifies with our spirit that we are God's children. Now if we are children, then we are heirs—heirs of God and co-heirs with Christ, if indeed we share in his sufferings in order that we may also share in his glory.

ROMANS 8:16–17 NIV

Wealthy citizens in first-century Rome who lacked an heir would often adopt a young slave boy as their son. Slaves often performed hard labor and suffered abuse. Their every moment was controlled by the needs of their master. But once they were adopted, slaves began a brand-new life as their father's heir. The ties to their old family were severed and their old debts forgiven. We too have been redeemed from our old lives of sin. The ties to darkness and death have been severed. We're heirs with Christ.

Father, help me to rejoice even in the sufferings of this life, because the glory of heaven far outweighs the pains I have now! Amen.

Day 306

Perfectly

Your kingdom is an everlasting kingdom, and your dominion endures through all generations. The LORD is trustworthy in all he promises and faithful in all he does.

PSALM 145:13 NIV

God's faithfulness to you never falters. It began before you were born and will last far beyond the day you die. Nothing you do, or don't do, can adversely affect His love and devotion. This kind of faithfulness can only come from God. Those who love you may promise they'll never let you down, but they're fallible. Just like you. Only God is perfect—and perfectly trustworthy. What He says, He does. Today, tomorrow, and always.

Dear Lord, forgive us for putting our trust in things other than You: in people, abilities, situations, money, habits, histories. All those things will fail us. Only You are the one true God, from everlasting to everlasting, faithful to every promise You have ever made. Amen.

Day 307

A Haven While in Transition

Be to me a rock of refuge, to which I may continually come.
Psalm 71:3 ESV

Moving to another location involves not only hard work but also emotional upheaval. Some families experience this regularly; others may only experience it once or twice in their family's life. Some never do.

But if you are in the process of moving or if you know someone who is, it is good to be reminded that uprooting and relocating isn't something simply done. It is complex. It affects almost every aspect of personal and family life.

Women have a strong need for security, for domestic constancy. Moving is a challenge to that need. The Word of God tells us that God is our refuge where we may come continually. That's good news, wherever we are currently living.

Lord, thank You for being a continuous refuge.
Give me strength and hope in my uprooted moments. Amen.

Day 308

Press On

Not that I have already obtained this or am already perfect, but I press on to make it my own, because Christ Jesus has made me his own.

PHILIPPIANS 3:12 ESV

Press on. These words conjure up the image of a difficult journey, a struggle to survive harsh conditions. But they also offer up the hope of a better destination. "Press on" seems to say that there's something promising up ahead, something worthy of the hardship, something worth striving for. We haven't reached perfection, nor will we in this world, but the apostle Paul urges, "Press on." When trials test your faith, choose trust. When illness threatens death, choose His life. When despair darkens your door, choose hope. When hate haunts your thoughts, choose love. Press on to His kingdom, beloved!

Father, You are my strength when I am weak. Fill me with the will to press on, right into Your arms. Amen.

Day 309

Pattern for Your Life

You should imitate me, just as I imitate Christ. I am so glad that you always keep me in your thoughts, and that you are following the teachings I passed on to you.
1 CORINTHIANS 11:1–2 NLT

Have you noticed that kids do as they see instead of as they're told? Our actions are much more powerful teachers than our words. Can you offer up this same advice to the believers around you? Are you confident enough in your walk to hold it up as an example to follow? Whether we say the words or not, our children and faith children are watching to see what we'll do. Our actions don't just affect us; they affect all those we are teaching by example.

Lord, make me a worthy example. I know that I'm not perfect, but teach me to pattern my life after Christ. Amen.

Day 310

Fixer-Upper

All of us who have had that veil removed can see and reflect the glory of the Lord. And the Lord—who is the Spirit—makes us more and more like him as we are changed into his glorious image.

2 CORINTHIANS 3:18 NLT

Our first house was a gem—but in the rough for sure. The stench cut you down as you crossed the threshold, and neighbors said the place needed a match not a makeover. But we gutted her practically to the studs and started over. Before Jesus, our lives are a lot like that house—smelly, dirty, broken down, and hopeless. But Jesus—He sees the promise of good bones, just like we did in that house. He sees us not for what we are but for what we could be with Him. His Holy Spirit can refurbish our dirty dysfunction and transform us into His ever-increasing glory.

Father, thank You for remaking me in You. Amen.

Day 311

Nothing Apart from God

All this have I tried and proved by wisdom. I said, I will be wise [independently of God]—but it was far from me.

ECCLESIASTES 7:23 AMPC

Culture often touts the wisdom of celebrities and CEOs and other influencers who are popular in the moment. Their words on how to build a business, make money, create a following, craft a brand, structure a portfolio, and more are printed, published, and quoted. Their interviews are sought after, and their names are desired for advertising. But if they seek to be wise independently of God, they will ultimately fail in the business of eternity.

Building a life and making decisions based on the solid wisdom of God is the key to lasting success. The wisdom writer of scripture was inspired to remind us that there is no true wisdom apart from Him.

Lord God, today I seek Your eternal wisdom. Amen.

Day 312

Wait in Hope

The eyes of the Lord are on those who fear him, on those whose hope is in his unfailing love. . . . We wait in hope for the Lord; he is our help and our shield.

Psalm 33:18, 20 NIV

When prosperity flows and you're whistling "Zip-a-Dee-Doo-Dah," it's simple to hope in God's love and trust His future for you, because that future seems pretty bright from where you're sitting. But God's unfailing love for us stretches further than this earthly lifespan, as do His plans. We like comfort, so it is natural that we want help and a shield on our terms. But God may have your long-term good in mind instead of your immediate comfort. Remember that His love never fails, and He may be teaching you to wait in hope no matter what. Where is God saying "wait" in your life?

Father, I put my hope in Your unfailing love, not in circumstances. Amen.

Day 313

Forged by Family

Our Lord, in all generations you have been our home.
Psalm 90:1 CEV

Your family is unique. You may be married, single, with kids or without. Parents, siblings, aunts, cousins. . .they're all part of the family God's placed you in. That family can be a testing ground for faith. That's because the more time you spend with people, the easier it is for them to rub you the wrong way—and vice versa. Consider what God wants to teach you through your family. Patience? Forgiveness? Grace? Don't put off until tomorrow what you could learn today.

Lord, we often forget to thank You: for our daily bread, for our homes and clothes and jobs, for our loved ones, for the breath that fills our lungs. Thank You also for the struggles we go through that You are using to conform us into the image of Christ. Amen.

Day 314

Calm in the Storm

He hushes the storm to a calm and to a gentle whisper, so that the waves of the sea are still.

Psalm 107:29 AMPC

Perhaps you have been on the water when a storm blew in. Today, we usually have advance warning of bad weather. In Bible times, they didn't. They relied more on their senses and their instincts honed from years of experience.

One of the well-known miracles of Jesus is the calming of the storm that arose on the Sea of Galilee. And how often we find ourselves in a sudden storm—a health crisis, a family emergency, a relationship drama, a ministry challenge, an emotional disruption. In these times, we can turn to the one who "hushes the storm." It may still howl around us, but in our spirits, He whispers gently and holds us securely.

Lord Jesus, You stilled the storm for the disciples; quiet mine today. Amen.

Day 315

Unoffendable

Since God chose you to be the holy people he loves, you must clothe yourselves with tenderhearted mercy, kindness, humility, gentleness, and patience. Make allowance for each other's faults, and forgive anyone who offends you. Remember, the Lord forgave you, so you must forgive others.

COLOSSIANS 3:12–13 NLT

Now that you belong to God, He wants you to live holy. But how can we robe ourselves with the virtues of God? That's a lofty goal, especially when grumbling is second nature. If you find fault with someone, remember that God has endless reasons to find fault with you too, but through Jesus, this tremendous debt is forgiven. Knowing this should lighten your spirits!

God, make me unoffendable in my patience. In Jesus' name, amen.

Day 316

Chosen for Power

"You will receive power when the Holy Spirit comes upon you. And you will be my witnesses, telling people about me everywhere—in Jerusalem, throughout Judea, in Samaria, and to the ends of the earth."

Acts 1:8 NLT

God doesn't make empty promises, and He never offers meaningless gifts. When Jesus left the earth after His resurrection, He promised the disciples that they wouldn't have to go it alone—and neither do you. When you're struggling to trust or exhaustion weights your limbs, when you just feel like you can't, there's hope—because *you* don't have to handle it. Jesus will. He promises that through the Holy Spirit, we can share in the power of God. The disciples were filled with power and traveled the known world spreading the gospel. They showed heroic courage in the face of grave circumstances—through God's power.

Lord, I need Your Spirit's power today. Amen.

Day 317

She Speaks Wisdom

When she speaks, her words are wise,
and she gives instructions with kindness.
PROVERBS 31:26 NLT

Have you ever lived to regret the deadly accuracy of your tongue? Undoing the damage once those lethal words are out can be impossible—like putting toothpaste back in the tube. But God has a different way, a path of holiness. He wants us to rein in our words. Through the instruction of the Holy Spirit, we can open our mouths, and instead of spewing poison, wisdom will flow out. We can offer encouragement and kindness through gentle and wise words to the people around us. God's wisdom teaches us that we don't always have to be first. Wisdom teaches us to love well.

Father, fill my words with wisdom. Prevent unholy things from leaving my mouth and injuring those around me. Instead, give me wisdom to build and not destroy. Amen.

Day 318

Inside and Out

God met me more than halfway, he freed me from my anxious fears. Look at him; give him your warmest smile. Never hide your feelings from him.

Psalm 34:4–5 MSG

God knows you inside and out. He knows how you feel, right here, right now. So why bother telling Him what's going on in your heart? Because that's how relationships grow. Sharing your personal struggles with a spouse or best friend is a sign of intimacy. It demonstrates your faith in his or her love for you. It also gives the other person an opportunity to offer comfort, help, and hope. God desires that same opportunity in your life.

Dear Father, we long to know You better; we long for the intimacy that David describes in this psalm. And You long for that too. You know every thought, desire, and struggle already, but You long for us to run to You with them—for our good and Your glory. Amen.

Day 319

Salted or Sweetened

You are a hiding place for me; you preserve me from trouble; you surround me with shouts of deliverance.

Psalm 32:7 ESV

Our grandmothers often made preserves—of fruits and vegetables. What was needed was a preserving agent to keep the fresh substance from decaying. Sometimes salt was used; other times, sugar was employed. And the wonderful result gave us delighted tummies for months to come.

God is into preserving His saints in times of trouble. Sometimes He uses salt—the trial irritates us but makes us better because of the action of the briny pain involved. Sometimes He works through pleasant means—protection from the worst, a miraculous answer. But either way, He is using the best means at that moment to preserve us and keep us fresh for eternity.

Heavenly Father, thank You for preserving me in the way You know is best right now. Amen.

Day 320

Trust the Anchor

This hope is a strong and trustworthy anchor for our souls. It leads us through the curtain into God's inner sanctuary. Jesus has already gone in there for us.
HEBREWS 6:19–20 NLT

In our day of air travel, we aren't as familiar with the imagery of anchors. But in the day when these words were penned, the average person knew the importance of an anchor. Ships were the major means of international transport, and many people to whom the New Testament epistles were written lived along sea routes. Anchors keep large ships from drifting in the water and secure them during stormy blasts.

Our hope in Christ is the anchor of our souls. When life's calamities pile on us, our trust in Him keeps us upright and secure.

Lord Jesus, I cast myself into Your keeping and trust You as a ship does its anchor. Amen.

Day 321

Believe

"I tell you the truth, unless you turn from your sins and become like little children, you will never get into the Kingdom of Heaven."
MATTHEW 18:3 NLT

Our little ones pray with childlike wonder. Everything seems possible because they frolic in a world of fairy tales and miracles unshaded by adult disappointment and devastation. But with God, believing that nothing is impossible doesn't have to fade with our childhood. Fully trusting Him isn't childish fancy. Take a moment and think about what's weighing on your mind—a broken relationship, a lost job, a difficult decision—and bring it to God with childlike faith that He is able to step into your circumstances with solutions you didn't think were possible, fully expecting His answer.

Father, I believe. Help me to pray as I did when I was a child, fully believing that You are able. Amen.

Day 322

No Holding Back

It was by faith that Abraham offered Isaac as a sacrifice when God was testing him. Abraham, who had received God's promises, was ready to sacrifice his only son, Isaac, even though God had told him, "Isaac is the son through whom your descendants will be counted." Abraham reasoned that if Isaac died, God was able to bring him back to life again. And in a sense, Abraham did receive his son back from the dead.

HEBREWS 11:17–19 NLT

What do you hold close to your heart? Your children? Your money or position? Are you willing to trust God with it, to prove your faith? Tough question. Abraham had faith that God would keep His promise through Isaac, so he raised the knife over his beloved son and trusted God to provide. The great news is that God actually did what He asked of Abraham. He gave us Jesus.

Father, search my heart and show me what I'm holding back from You, who gave everything for me. Amen.

Day 323

Heavenly Ambitions

"Those who have it very hard for doing right are happy, because the holy nation of heaven is theirs."

MATTHEW 5:10 NLV

Most of us learn from an early age that taking the easy road will usually result in more work later. Experience quickly educates us that there are only two ways to do something: right and again. But even when we choose the right way, trouble can pounce. Job definitely didn't anticipate the travesty that visited him. But he was certain of his Redeemer. And we can be too. Joy can well in your soul when you keep an eternal focus. This life is short, but eternity is long. And a glorious home in heaven awaits after the troubles of this world are behind us.

Father, fill my heart with joy when I suffer for doing the right thing. In the long run, I will win! Amen.

Day 324

Control and Clarity

But even if we don't feel at ease, God is greater than our feelings, and he knows everything.

1 JOHN 3:20 CEV

Do you regard your emotions as friend or foe? Your answer may depend on how much they control your life. God created you as a woman, an emotional being. Your wide range of emotions—including empathy, anger, compassion, joy, sorrow, and fear—all help you assess situations and decide on appropriate action. But it takes God's wisdom to balance the power of your emotions. When emotions run high, ask God for control and clarity before you act.

Lord, when I am ruled by emotion, I am not being ruled by You. Forgive me for allowing my feelings and thoughts to toss me like waves. I long to be ruled by You so that my emotions become a rich source of praise and a gift to share with others. Amen.

Day 325

Fuel for Life

Three different times I begged the Lord to take it away. Each time he said, "My grace is all you need. My power works best in weakness." So now I am glad to boast about my weaknesses, so that the power of Christ can work through me.

2 CORINTHIANS 12:8–9 NLT

It has been said that grace is the Christian's fuel for life. There are two types of grace—one is the merciful favor of salvation through the blood of Christ, and the other is the divine enablement to meet the challenges of life. It is the latter kind that Paul references in the scripture above.

Grace, the gift of strength from God, is available to us anywhere, anytime, in any measure. We can never exhaust the supply. We can never ask too often. In fact, we usually fail to ask for enough of it.

Today, in your moment of calamity, cry out to God for grace. It's there.

Father, I depend on heaven's fuel today. In Jesus' name, amen.

Day 326

A Matter of Poise

Strength and dignity are her clothing and
her position is strong and secure.
PROVERBS 31:25 AMPC

In previous centuries, young girls were often sent to "finishing schools" where they were "finished" or polished, receiving careful instruction in refinement and proper social graces. Poise would have been at the top of the list. It was demonstrated by actions like always speaking in even tones, even in times of excitement or strain, and in never turning to stare or acting baffled by another's social faux pas.

Today, we still value another woman's ability to keep her cool and act with strength and dignity in difficult situations. The Bible also praises this ability and tells us at the end of the chapter that dependence on the Lord makes these virtues possible.

God, I want to be a woman of poise even in calamity. Give me that kind of strength. Amen.

Day 327

I Want to Be with You

Make a clean heart in me, O God. Give me a new spirit that will not be moved. Do not throw me away from where You are. And do not take Your Holy Spirit from me.

PSALM 51:10–11 NLV

Moms the world over are known as the glue that holds families together, because they understand an important truth: one of the most satisfying feelings is being together with someone you love. When we wander from God, we forget how amazing it is to spend time in God's presence. But when we come to our senses, we realize that our spirit longs to come home to Him.

Lord, I've tried doing my own thing and pleasing myself. The only thing I've gained is misery. I'm ready to please You, Father. I just want to be where You are. Show me how to live for You. Amen.

Day 328

Begin to Understand

Do not speak evil against one another. . . . There is only one lawgiver and judge, he who is able to save and to destroy. But who are you to judge your neighbor?

JAMES 4:11–12 ESV

When life is going our way, we can morph into arrogant creatures. Our advice chafes: "If you would just do things my way, life would be better for you." But we must drop the judgment because, in truth, no one's circumstances are identical to ours. Have you considered the other person's secret hardships? Instead of cold platitudes and misguided advice, maybe offer to help and get a firsthand feel for the weight of their load. If you walk in their shoes for a bit, you might find yourself feeling more compassionate about their choices.

Father, I sometimes judge others without understanding what their life is like. Please give me more love and less condemnation. Amen.

Day 329

Believe Every Word

We always thank God that when you heard the Word of God from us, you believed it. You did not receive it as from men, but you received it as the Word of God.

1 THESSALONIANS 2:13 NLV

We can't see gravity, but we know with absolute certainty that it's as real as the dirt we stand on. We recognize through experience, sometimes the painful kind, that what goes up must come down. And though we can't see God with our eyes, we *can* see Him with the eyes of our faith. We know the wonderful things He has done for us. We can count the answers to prayer, feel His comforting arms, and experience His peace. Take Him at His Word today. He is here. He is never leaving. And His love surrounds you.

Father, I know You're here even though I can't see You. I believe everything You've told me. Amen.

Day 330

God’s Family

May the God who gives endurance and encouragement give you the same attitude of mind toward each other that Christ Jesus had.

Romans 15:5 NIV

God’s family is like your own biological family. You’re bound to get along better with some members than with others. When God paints a picture of unity among His people, it doesn’t mean disagreements and misunderstandings disappear. It simply means that the faith you share will encourage you to work through any problems that arise. Together, as God’s family, you can learn what love really looks like, encouraging one another toward growth while helping smooth out each other’s rough edges.

Dear God, today I pray for my church. It is so easy to be divided by small differences. Help us to live and love in unity and peace and walk in step with You. You are infinite, Lord; there is room at the foot of the cross for everyone. Amen.

Day 331

Waiting Out the Storm

Be merciful to me, O God, be merciful to me, for in you my soul takes refuge; in the shadow of your wings I will take refuge, till the storms of destruction pass by.

Psalm 57:1 ESV

If you picture in your mind a place of refuge, what would it be?

In earlier days, almost every farm in the blustery region of the country had a storm cellar, a subterranean shelter with an entrance often covered by a door and leading downward by steps into the earth. There, the family would retreat when a cyclone was spotted on the horizon, taking refuge until the storms passed.

There may be a twister headed your way today. Head for your refuge in Christ and wait out the storm in His strength.

Lord of Refuge, I run to You today.
Hide me in the shadow of Your wings. Amen.

Day 332

Leaning on the Right Support

The Lord is my strength and my song;
he has become my salvation.
Psalm 118:14 ESV

One of the common maladies in later years is back pain. After supporting our spines and helping us walk and lift and perform all manner of other actions, the back often lets us know that it is tired and sometimes injured. The skeletal structure and muscular system that God designed are amazing, but wear and tear and sometimes an unwise move or two can cause them to malfunction. The support we thought we had is gone.

Often in times of duress, we find that our earthly networks of support are incapable of holding our weight. They malfunction and let us down. But the strength we gain from our trust in God is unfailing. It will hold us forever.

Lord God, thank You for the support I find in Your strength. I lean on You today. Amen.

Day 333

Dollars

Remember the Lord *your God, for it is he who gives you the ability to produce wealth.*
Deuteronomy 8:18 niv

A sense of entitlement comes with a paycheck. You earned it, so you get to choose how to spend it, right? But have you ever stopped to consider how the way God created you impacts your ability to earn a living? Take a moment right now to thank God for His part in your financial picture. Ask Him to give you wisdom, self-control, and a spirit of generosity as you choose how to use every dollar you receive.

Lord, I have never wanted for anything. I have always been fed, housed, clothed, and loved. Every time I have felt a lack was really because I had turned away from You, away from the joyful discipline of counting my blessings. Right now, I recommit to giving thanks. Amen.

Day 334

My Light

Through him all things were made; without him nothing was made that has been made. In him was life, and that life was the light of all mankind. The light shines in the darkness, and the darkness has not overcome it.

John 1:3–5 NIV

Every year on Christmas morning, I wake up before the first blush of dawn to sit in the stillness. The kids are sleeping peacefully with the joy of anticipation sweetening their dreams. I snuggle into my favorite chair with my coffee and read about the humble birth of Jesus—the magnificent Savior of a world in need. This year as I looked at the twinkling lights glowing on our tree, I thought about the light that shines in my darkness—my hope, my life, my rescue and strength. What if every day began as this one?

Father, make every morning a holy contemplation of the light You bring to my world. Amen.

Day 335

A True Daughter

No discipline seems pleasant at the time, but painful. Later on, however, it produces a harvest of righteousness and peace.

HEBREWS 12:11 NIV

We can all probably dredge up a few stories of youthful folly that end with ". . .then my parents grounded me for a month." Although no parent is perfect, we correct our children because we love them and don't want to see them lead foolish and pain-filled lives. God disciplines us when we step out of line too. And the rewards are high: righteousness and peace through learning to go the right way. And remember the best news: God's discipline proves our place as His children. "If you are not disciplined. . .then you are not legitimate, not true sons and daughters at all" (Hebrews 12:8 NIV).

Loving Father, thank You for loving me enough to correct my way. A little pain now will pay off in righteousness and peace. Amen.

Day 336
Avoiding Worry

[Wisdom's] ways are highways of pleasantness,
and all her paths are peace.
PROVERBS 3:17 AMPC

"Don't worry; be happy" used to be a popular catchphrase. But in the middle of our distresses, peace seems far away. When we receive shocking news or experience an unexpected crisis, our immediate tendency is toward anxiety and fear. This is a natural human reaction. The only way to change that visceral response is with the solid help of the Lord. When we depend on His wisdom, we can move toward peace.

The Bible tells us that His peace comes from looking at life through His perspective and by trusting His providential care and His sovereign will at work in our lives.

Heavenly Father, the only way I can avoid worry is to trust Your wisdom about my future. By Your grace, I do that today. Amen.

Day 337

A True Paradise

If we confess our sins to God, he can always be trusted to forgive us and take our sins away.
1 JOHN 1:9 CEV

Faith and forgiveness are two sides of the same coin. You cannot hold on to one without embracing the other. If you believe Jesus loves you so much that He would pay the penalty for your sins with His own life, then you must also believe that He wouldn't hold those sins against you any longer. If you're feeling guilty, talk to God. Your feelings are not always truth-tellers. God's forgiveness is what makes spending eternity with Him a true paradise.

Father, thank You for the size of Your forgiveness: as far as the east is from the west, as deep as the ocean, as wide as the sky. And You don't just forgive, but You take our sins away as though they had never been. Help us to rest and rejoice in Your undeserved mercy. Amen.

Day 338
Set Free

Don't you know that when you offer yourselves to someone as obedient slaves, you are slaves of the one you obey— whether you are slaves to sin, which leads to death, or to obedience, which leads to righteousness? But thanks be to God that, though you used to be slaves to sin, you have come to obey from your heart the pattern of teaching that has now claimed your allegiance. You have been set free from sin and have become slaves to righteousness.

Romans 6:16–18 NIV

We all serve something. We spend our days building legacies and fortunes, chasing dreams, and sometimes just running after our own pleasure. Evaluate the ways you spend your time, your money, and all the things that are important to you. A slave lives to do the bidding of her master. What things are mastering you?

Father, teach me to obey willingly and joyfully. Amen.

Day 339

Joy in the Coming Dawn

*Satisfy us in the morning with your unfailing love,
that we may sing for joy and be glad all our days.*
Psalm 90:14 NIV

Dark times sometimes descend over our lives. Many Christians have lived through bleak periods in history, and we're not guaranteed ease and comfort either. But the black night of our current situation gives way to the light of morning when we're enfolded by the steadfast love of God. Because we are players in the greatest love story in history, the rescue of a doomed people, our songs of praise to our great God can still reign in our hearts in spite of desperate circumstances. Our hope cannot be crushed. Our joy cannot be extinguished. Because of Jesus.

Heavenly Father, when I'm passing through dark valleys, assaulted by difficulties, keep my hope and faith in the eternal sunrise of dwelling in Your presence. Amen.

Day 340

Generational Loyalty

Then Jonathan said to David, "Go in peace,
because we have sworn both of us in the name of the
Lord, saying, 'The Lord shall be between me and you,
and between my offspring and your offspring, forever.'"
1 Samuel 20:42 ESV

The friendship of David and Jonathan is an enduring example of loyalty and tenacity. King Saul was obsessed with killing David, ending what he considered to be a threat to his throne and his legacy through the prince Jonathan. Yet despite the fact that he and his sons would not reign, Jonathan was David's best friend and even an ally against his father's schemes.

Probably none of your friendships have this kind of backdrop, yet there are many strains that come against friendship. Resolve that you will be the kind of friend who pledges faithfulness even to your children's generation.

Lord, give me understanding and integrity
so I may be a true friend. Amen.

Day 341

Get Her to Jesus

And they came, bringing to him a paralytic carried by four men. And when they could not get near him because of the crowd, they removed the roof above him, and when they had made an opening, they let down the bed on which the paralytic lay.

MARK 2:3–4 ESV

These guys didn't let the inconvenience of the hardship or the weird looks from other people stop them not only from carrying his bed but also from taking apart the roof to lower his bed into the house.

As a friend, there may be ways you can serve that will not be easy or convenient. You may feel embarrassed as you do what is best for your friend, despite what others think. But getting her to Jesus is what counts. Don't let anything stop you.

Lord, give me wisdom to know how best to serve my friend in a way that brings her to You. Amen.

Day 342

My Hope and Portion

The steadfast love of the Lord *never ceases; his mercies never come to an end; they are new every morning; great is your faithfulness. "The* Lord *is my portion," says my soul, "therefore I will hope in him."*

Lamentations 3:22–24 ESV

We see the new year as a fresh start, but what's significant about a changing date? Why do we feel so empowered to start losing weight or kick a bad habit when the calendar flips? We tell ourselves *next year* will be better. *Next year* I'll change. But what about today? We don't have to wait until the start of a new year to talk to God about our mistakes. And scripture reminds us that there's a ray of hope: His mercy is new every morning. Make Him your portion and hope every day.

Lord, living for You is all I need today and every day. Amen.

Day 343

The Ultimate Gain

I once thought these things were valuable, but now I consider them worthless because of what Christ has done. Yes, everything else is worthless when compared with the infinite value of knowing Christ Jesus my Lord. For his sake I have discarded everything else, counting it all as garbage, so that I could gain Christ.

PHILIPPIANS 3:7–8 NLT

In Paul's accounting, we have assets and liabilities. But after he met Jesus, what he thought were his assets—his position, power, and obedience to the law—were actually losses. Not only were they worthless, but they were dragging him down. Instead, he discovered that what he thought was a total loss—a crucified Messiah—was the ultimate gain. Do you need to reevaluate where you're finding value? Jesus said, "What does it profit a man to gain the whole world and forfeit his soul?" (Mark 8:36 ESV).

Father, keep me from putting value in worthless things. Experiencing Jesus' love and friendship is the unrivaled win. In Jesus' name, amen.

Day 344

The Right Motive

"These people honor me with their lips,
but their hearts are far from me."
MATTHEW 15:8 NIV

Do you ever find yourself following God's ways literally but ignoring the deeper meaning behind His commands? I have definitely babysat for a friend or helped my husband clean out the garage—while grumbling to myself the whole time. Jesus was asked once what the greatest commandment was, and He said this: " 'Love the Lord your God with all your heart and with all your soul and with all your mind.' This is the first and greatest commandment. And the second is like it: 'Love your neighbor as yourself' " (Matthew 22:37–39 NIV). Love is the greatest commandment. Our outward actions become meaningless in the absence of love.

Father, please forgive me for doing the right thing outwardly without love in my heart. Teach me to love like Jesus. Amen.

Day 345

Stay Alert!

Keep awake! Watch at all times. The devil is working against you. He is walking around like a hungry lion with his mouth open. He is looking for someone to eat.

1 Peter 5:8 NLV

Make no mistake, Satan is not your friend. Scripture tells us that in his wake are stolen hopes, death, and destruction. He knows that you've been chosen as God's child, and his biggest pleasure is causing pain or offering you pleasure and position to lure you away from God. Stay alert to your thoughts and motivations because the enemy is actively working against you. Any time he can cause a Christian to stumble, he hammers another dent in God's reputation. What circumstances have you allowed to plant a seed of doubt about God's love for you?

Father, give me wisdom to be as wise as a serpent and as gentle as a dove. Amen.

Day 346

Immediately. Completely. Eternally.

Be even-tempered, content with second place, quick to forgive an offense.
COLOSSIANS 3:12–13 MSG

When you put your faith in God, the very first thing He does is forgive you. He doesn't overlook what you've done. He forgives it. Immediately. Completely. Eternally. Choosing to follow His example isn't always easy. But it's always right. When others offend you, don't let your forgiveness hinge on their apology or repentance. You can wisely set boundaries and still offer forgiveness. Ask God to help you forgive before another's fault can fester into a painful, distracting grudge.

Dear Lord, forgive me for the sins I hold against others. Forgive me for the anger and lack of forgiveness in my heart. Remind me how much I have been forgiven and extend that same grace to those who have hurt me. Only Your Spirit can enable that in me. Amen.

Day 347

Determined to Do Good

And let us not grow weary of doing good, for in due season we will reap, if we do not give up. So then, as we have opportunity, let us do good to everyone, and especially to those who are of the household of faith.

GALATIANS 6:9–10 ESV

How we treat others is an indication of how seriously we take our love for the Lord. Jesus told us that to love our neighbor as ourselves demonstrates our surrendered love for God (Matthew 22:36–40). The integrity of our friendships matters.

The apostle Paul, under divine inspiration, wrote that we should not give up doing what is good to everyone. Today, be determined to bless your friends, speak truthfully with them, and point them to Christ. Friendship is a reflection of our biblical understanding. Your friends need you.

Father God, because I love You, I make a deliberate choice to love others. In Jesus' name, amen.

Day 348

Never Forget

Praise the Lord, O my soul. And forget
none of His acts of kindness.
PSALM 103:2 NLV

Do you need to revitalize a dreary perspective and exchange negativity for a more positive outlook? Following Christ doesn't mean you'll skip through life, happy at every turn. But the glass-half-empty mentality can become a bad habit. Sure, unfortunate things happen, and sometimes nothing seems to be going our way, but a new perspective can keep you from sounding like Chicken Little. Simply remember the kindnesses of God—make a list, write a poem, post them on your mirror, sing about them in the shower. Never forget that you were dead but are now alive!

Father, help me to keep things in perspective. Even when I seem to come out with the short end of the stick too often, I am abundantly blessed. Amen.

Day 349

Light to My Path

Your word is a lamp to my feet and a light to my path. I have sworn an oath and confirmed it, to keep your righteous rules.
PSALM 119:105–106 ESV

We navigate our homes with no problem when the lights are on. But when a howling windstorm knocks out the power in the dead of night, our shins take a beating as we grope through the darkness for a flashlight. Are you confused and seeking answers? Don't fall for the enemy's deception that you don't have time to read scripture or it's too difficult to understand. Turn on the light. Pick up your Bible—dust it off if you have to. Your heavenly Father promises you will gain understanding and direction in your choices.

Father, thank You for giving us Your Word. Give me understanding and discernment through studying Your ways. Amen.

Day 350

Free to Be

I will walk in freedom, for I have devoted myself to your commandments.

PSALM 119:45 NLT

Without rules, what sounds like freedom can be chaos. Take driving, for instance. You need a license to operate a motor vehicle. That's not because the DMV is worried about your being a woman driver. It's because traffic flows "freer" when everyone knows and follows the rules. The same is true when living a life of faith. God's commandments help us build stronger relationships. We're freer to be ourselves—and love God and others well—when we follow His rules.

Dear Lord, thank You that Your Word brings abundant life, not restriction. Your fences bring us complete freedom within the bounds of Your will. Your commandments were only ever given for our good, to point us to the Savior, Jesus Christ, who obeys perfectly. Amen.

Day 351

Redeemed Flaws

Who are you, a mere human being, to argue with God? Should the thing that was created say to the one who created it, "Why have you made me like this?"
ROMANS 9:20 NLT

Every woman has them. Flaws. Facial flaws. Figure flaws. Beauty flaws.

When we look at ourselves in the mirror, we usually dismiss the good points and focus on the problems. We can't even seem to see what's right because we are so ashamed of what's wrong.

God, our Creator, wants us to know that there is hope for our beauty because He created it. The flaws that are a result of fallenness cannot annihilate His good design. We may not see the perfection of us until we get to heaven, but we must believe it is there!

Designer God, I know You have made me and that my flaws will be redeemed someday in Your presence. Amen.

Day 352

Worthy and Redeemed

You know that God paid a ransom to save you from the empty life you inherited from your ancestors. And it was not paid with mere gold or silver, which lose their value.

1 PETER 1:18 NLT

Comparing ourselves to one another and guesstimating our worth are activities we engage in from girlhood. We easily fall into the idea that those who have a certain waist circumference or certain hair color or brand-name clothing or whatever are worth more. It makes sense to our childly minds—she is prettier than I am, and she has nicer shoes; therefore, she is more important.

God has a very different scale for determining our worth.

1. Our creation—He made us: He only makes good things.
2. Our redemption—He gave the costly gift of His Son.

Both of these reasons say we are of ultimate worth to Him.

Heavenly Father, I look to You to determine my value today. Amen.

Day 353

Where's Your Treasure?

"Do not store up for yourselves treasures on earth, where moths and vermin destroy, and where thieves break in and steal. But store up for yourselves treasures in heaven, where moths and vermin do not destroy, and where thieves do not break in and steal. For where your treasure is, there your heart will be also."

MATTHEW 6:19–21 NIV

Many beautiful mansions have fallen into ruins with the passage of time. They may have been the cherished homes of wealthy and influential people in days gone by, but with disuse and disrepair, their expansive floors lose their sheen and once-fashionable paper peels from their walls. Don't hope and trust in fleeting earthly possessions. Where is your treasure? Are you chasing things—cars, clothes, popularity—or does God hold first place in your life?

Father, teach me to serve others in love. I won't let passing possessions turn my eyes from You. Amen.

Day 354

Always and Forever

"I the Lord do not change."
Malachi 3:6 NIV

Anne Frank, the brave young girl who hid from the Nazis with her family in an attic, wrote, "[If] you try to improve yourself at the start of each new day. . . , you achieve quite a lot in the course of time. Anyone can do this, it costs nothing and is certainly very helpful." Change can be good. We gain experience and grow and develop good character. For us, change is unavoidable. But God never changes. He is always God—always good, always there, and always keeps His promises. This is great news for us! We can be sure that He is faithful and won't change His mind about our adoption as His beloved daughters.

Father, it gives me great comfort and courage to know that You are the same yesterday, today, and forever. But continue to shape me into a daughter who pleases You. Amen.

Day 355

Key to Freedom

The Scriptures declare that we are all prisoners of sin, so we receive God's promise of freedom only by believing in Jesus Christ.

Galatians 3:22 NLT

Imagine being locked in prison for years. You're guilty, hopeless, and helpless. Then a beloved friend volunteers to take your place. You're set free as another woman takes your punishment as her own. How much do you value the cost of your freedom? In essence, this is what Christ did for you. When you place your faith in Him, you're handed the key to freedom. Honor Jesus' gift by living a life worthy of such sacrifice.

Lord, I would live differently if there actually was another woman in jail in my place. I would continually tell of her love and sacrifice for me. Her praises would always be on my lips. You went to jail for me, Jesus! Whom the Son sets free is free indeed. Amen.

Day 356

Honoring Others

Love one another with brotherly affection.
Outdo one another in showing honor.
Romans 12:10 ESV

Being a person who respects others is a worthwhile reputation.

There are many things that pull at the fabric of society; lack of respect is one of them. When people neglect or refuse to respect one another because of differences of background or opinion or ethnicity or other reasons, the culture deteriorates. Genuine respect fosters civil behavior and logical conversations and compromise on issues that matter to all.

You can be a woman who is known for her respect for others. Your friends and acquaintances and neighbors should have no doubt that you will honor them as human beings even if you don't agree on every point of life. Jesus honored people; we should do the same.

Father God, remind me that every single person is a reflection of Your image; help me to honor everyone. Amen.

Day 357

Running Free

Therefore, since we are surrounded by such a great cloud of witnesses, let us throw off everything that hinders and the sin that so easily entangles. And let us run with perseverance the race marked out for us.

HEBREWS 12:1 NIV

Much to the frustration of gardeners everywhere, dandelions grow right back unless you dig up the root. What sins are crowding out your joy? Beloved, we all mess up, and when we do, God's grace has us covered. But God also desires you to overcome the sins that bring grief to your life and to your Father's heart. Do you stumble often into anger, gossip, or jealousy? What root is motivating this behavior? Selfishness? Fear? Pride? Allow God's Word to yank out the deep tendrils of sin strangling your new life in Christ.

Father, lay bare the root cause of my sin.
Give me strength through Your Spirit to win victory. Amen.

Day 358

Peace in the Storm

Jesus was in the stern, sleeping on a cushion. The disciples woke him and said to him, "Teacher, don't you care if we drown?" He got up, rebuked the wind and said to the waves, "Quiet! Be still!" Then the wind died down and it was completely calm. He said to his disciples, "Why are you so afraid? Do you still have no faith?"

MARK 4:38–40 NIV

Do you live your life like you know God is in control? Jesus wasn't sleeping in the boat out of carelessness about His well-being. His peace was anchored in trust. Usually we pray for God to take away whatever hard circumstances we're in, and sometimes He does, but sometimes He allows the storm to rage on and calms His child instead.

Father, whether You calm my storms or fill me with peace while the world falls apart around me, I trust in You. Amen.

Day 359

Creation Sings

The heavens declare the glory of God; the skies proclaim the work of his hands. Day after day they pour forth speech. . . . Their voice goes out into all the earth, their words to the ends of the world.

PSALM 19:1–2, 4 NIV

It's your birthday, and your favorite triple-chocolate cake awaits! You know that scrumptious confection didn't bake itself any more than the universe created itself. And the note says, "Enjoy!" It's evidence that your husband thought about you, baked your favorite cake, and loves you. In just this way, we can know God is there. The Bible says that God's creation cries out His existence with a clear voice. Stroll through nature today. Find some insects, a budding plant, or a spiderweb. Where do you see God's goodness, love, and power in His creation?

Lord, Your creation shouts Your glory and is irrefutable evidence of Your existence. Amen.

Day 360

Anew

The faithful love of the LORD *never ends!*
His mercies never cease. Great is his faithfulness;
his mercies begin afresh each morning.
LAMENTATIONS 3:22–23 NLT

We all blow it. We let anger turn our words into weapons. We fall back into patterns we vowed we'd never repeat. We feel ashamed of ourselves as wives, mothers, or friends. But this is another minute, another morning, another chance to begin anew. Faith can break a cycle of regrettable yesterdays—if we let it. God offers forgiveness and a fresh start to all who ask. He never tires of us bringing our brokenness to Him.

Lord, when You designed the world to turn on its axis, You gave us a picture of Your heart. Every day You paint the sky with beauty; every day darkness turns to dawn. We praise You for those reminders of how You bring light out of darkness and beauty out of ashes. Amen.

Day 361

Always the Same

But You remain the same, and Your years shall have no end.

PSALM 102:27 AMPC

God is the only entity in the universe who is always exactly the same. He has the supernatural divine quality of never changing. We are constantly changing in big and little ways; some are barely perceptible to others while some are the first thing people notice.

Treating others the same whenever we see them is a wonderful reputation. If a woman is moody—sometimes cheerful and talkative and then sometimes withdrawn and quiet—others will never quite know how they should approach her. The people we love to be around always greet us, make us feel important, and show by their smiles that they are glad to see us. Let's strive for that reputation.

O God, I'm glad You don't change. Help me to be consistent in treating others well. Amen.

Day 362

Live in His Presence

[Anna] never left the temple but worshiped night and day, fasting and praying. Coming up to [Joseph, Mary, and Jesus] at that very moment, she gave thanks to God and spoke about the child to all who were looking forward to the redemption of Jerusalem.

LUKE 2:37–38 NIV

Anna was a prophetess at the time of Jesus' birth. Scripture tells us that she was married for seven years and then lived as a widow until she was eighty-four years old. Even though she suffered heartbreak as a young woman, she chose to spend her days in the temple, continually present with her Lord. Anna was God's chosen vessel to share the news of Jesus' birth with those at the temple who were waiting for the Messiah. How can you bring God into every moment of your day and share the joyous news of Jesus?

Father, may I never leave Your company. Amen.

Day 363

Chosen

God has chosen you. You are holy and loved by Him.

COLOSSIANS 3:12 NLV

Sister, we've all felt unwanted, left out, or overlooked at some point in our lives. We've all experienced the painful burn that scorches our face when we believe we're insignificant or irrelevant in the seemingly happy crowd of popular people. But don't believe this insidious lie of the enemy—you're never unwanted. Beloved, you have been chosen. You are wanted by the great God of this universe. Not only are you wanted, but you are loved ecstatically by Him—no strings attached. When you feel insignificant, lonely, or depressed, remember that your Father loves you. He picked you especially, because He sees the unique way He designed you.

Heavenly Father, protect my mind from dangerous lies. Help me always to trust that Your love for me is without bounds. In Jesus' precious name, amen.

Day 364

An Inside Job

We look inside, and what we see is that anyone united with the Messiah gets a fresh start, is created new. The old life is gone; a new life emerges!
2 CORINTHIANS 5:17 MSG

Faith is the ultimate makeover. But it doesn't hide who you are with a lift or tuck here and a fresh coat of foundation there. This makeover isn't external—it's eternal. And it's totally an inside job. Jesus referred to it as being "born again." Those old habits, regrets, and mistakes are behind you. Your past is forgiven and your future is empowered by God's Spirit working through you. Let go of yesterday and grab hold of God's promise for today!

Dear Lord, thank You for this incredible truth. We are being made new—the old "us" has no power anymore. The Spirit that is in us now has immeasurably more power than the desires and fears that ruled us before we believed. We praise You, Lord, for fresh starts and new life. Amen.

Day 365

Uncommon Honesty

Therefore, having put away falsehood, let each one of you speak the truth with his neighbor, for we are members one of another.
EPHESIANS 4:25 ESV

The old saying goes that "Honesty is the best policy." And a reputation of honest dealing is one to be prized.

In our grandparents' day, a man's word was solid. And honesty was the finest commodity for a business.

While honesty is still valued and expressed today in our culture, a lack of public recognition of a moral code like the Ten Commandments has led to greater dishonesty in general, even in ways that many consider common for everyone.

If you can be known as a woman who always tells the truth, you will have a reputation worth keeping.

Dear Lord, prick my conscience when I get near to shading the truth, and help me to value honesty. In Jesus' name, amen.

Scripture Index

OLD TESTAMENT

Proverbs

NEW TESTAMENT

Daily Inspiration for a Woman's Spirit!

Daily 3-Minute Devotions for Women

This delightful daily devotional packs a powerful dose of comfort, encouragement, and inspiration into just-right-sized readings that will easily fit into your busy day. Each biblically faithful reading will speak to your heart and comfort your soul.

Flexible Casebound / 979-8-89151-022-7

Find This and More from Barbour Publishing at Your Favorite Bookstore or www.barbourbooks.com

BARBOUR PUBLISHING